ADAM SEDGWICK

Geologist and Dalesman, 1785–1873

A biography in twelve themes

Geology

In that small town* was born a worthy wight
(His honest townsmen well approve his worth),
Whose mind has pierced the solid crust of earth,
And roam's undaunted in the nether night.
His thought a quenchless incorporeal light,
Has thrid the labryinth of a world unknown,
Where the old Gorgon time has turn'd to stone
Long thorny snake and monstrous lithophyte.
Long may'st thou wander in that deep obscure,
And issuing thence, good sage, bring with thee still
That honest face, where truth and goodness shine;
Right in thy creed, as all thy life is pure.
And yet if certain persons had their will
The fate of Galileo would be thine.

Hartley Coleridge
1796–1849

* Dent

ADAM SEDGWICK
Geologist and Dalesman, 1785–1873

A biography in twelve themes

by Colin Speakman

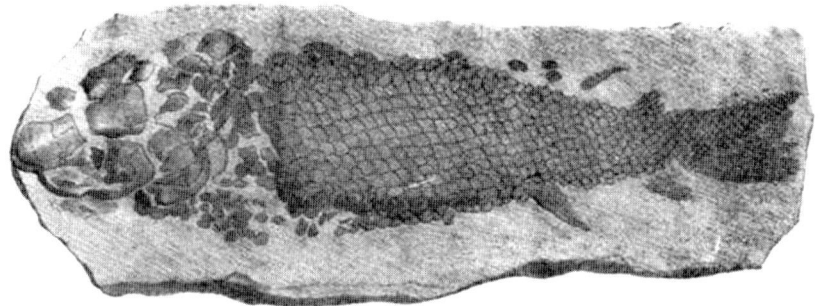

The fossil fish *Thursius macrolepidotus* (Sedgwick & Murchison) of the Devonian rocks of Caithness, Scotland, discovered and first described by Adam Sedgwick and Roderick Impey Murchison, Transactions of the Geological Society of London, Series 2, Volume 3, 1829.

Published jointly by
Gritstone Writers Co-operative Ltd.
and The Yorkshire Geological Society

First published in 1982 by Broad Oak Press Limited,
together with The Geological Society of London
and Trinity College, Cambridge.

Facsimile edition with new introduction published in 2018 by
Gritstone Writers Co-operative,
Birchcliffe Centre,
Hebden Bridge,
West Yorkshire
HX7 8DG
www.gritstone.coop

In partnership with
The Yorkshire Geological Society
www.yorksgeolsoc.org.uk

ISBN 978-0-9955609-4-9
© Colin Speakman except where stated

All rights reserved. No part of this publication may be re-produced, stored in a retrieval system or transmitted, in any form or by any means, electronic, mechanical photocopying, recording or otherwise without prior permission.

This edition typeset by Carnegie Book Production
Printed and bound in Great Britain by Jellyfish Solutions

For Arthur Raistrick, a latter day Sedgwick

The Yorkshire Geological Society

Founded in 1837, the YGS was the first geological society in northern England, and is a registered charity (Charity No. 220014). The Society promotes and records the results of research in geosciences in northern England, delivered through public lectures and field meetings, and publication of peer-reviewed scientific papers in the Society's internationally respected journal, "Proceedings of the Yorkshire Geological Society". The Society also publishes a range of other books and field guides on the geology and landscapes of northern England, aimed at both an amateur and professional readership.

The Society's lectures and field meetings cover a range of topical earth science issues, classic rock exposures and landscapes in northern England. Attendance is free to members and guests. Information on how to join the YGS and its programme of events and publications are available on the Society's website, www.yorksgeolsoc.org.uk

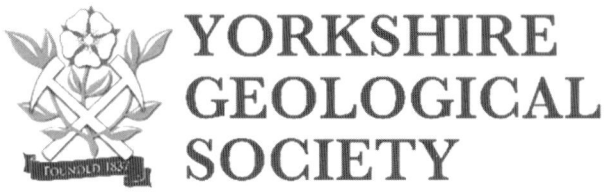

Contents

	Preface	ix
	List of Illustrations and Sources	xi
	Acknowledgements	xiii
1	The Granite Fountain	1
2	Adam o' th' Parsons	5
3	The Statesman of Dent	15
4	John Dawson of Garsdale	36
5	Cambridge: a crisis of identity	46
6	The making of a geologist	57
7	Controversy I: Cambrian versus Silurian	74
8	'I can only fire your imagination'	86
9	Controversy II: The Darwinian Revolution	100
10	The Prince and the Radical	112
11	Cowgill Chapel	123
12	The interpreter of a landscape	133
	References and Bibliography	139
	Index	143

'the wild and secluded little dale of Dent, the birthplace of our
Sedgwick, who, "long as yonder hills
Shall lift their heads inviolate"
will be named among the worthies of Yorkshire and honoured
among the most eminent geologists of the age.'
John Phillips

'The first of men'
Sir Roderick Impey Murchison

'One of the best field geologists of all time.'
W. F. Cannon

Preface

Adam Sedgwick was born in 1785 in the village of Dent in the Yorkshire Dales, son of the local parson. Through hard work and scholarship, he went to Trinity College Cambridge to eventually become a Fellow of the College. After struggling to find his true vocation he unexpectedly became Woodwardian Professor of Geology at Cambridge University and his new-found interest in the science eventually led him to become one of the most remarkable and influential geologists and teachers in 19th century England.

Sedgwick was not only one of the most brilliant field geologists of all time, but a teacher whose writing and lectures had a profound influence on generations of professional and amateur geologists and botanists. One of his more influential pupils was Charles Darwin, though in his later years Professor Sedgwick became a bitter and often controversial opponent of what he saw as the undermining of his Christian beliefs by Darwinian theories of Evolution. A friend and occasional walking companion of the poet William Wordsworth, he also became a close associate and friend of both Prince Albert and Queen Victoria. He went on to work with Prince Albert to bring about major reforms in university teaching in England and supported the Queen after Albert's untimely death. But even with his royal connections, he always remained true to his native Dentdale, a local benefactor and supporter, and through his writing, a brilliant recorder of life in this Dales community at a time of profound economic and social change.

List of Illustrations and Sources

Front Cover: Howgill Fells and Dentdale from Barbon Fells, North Yorkshire. Photo courtesy British Geological Survey © Natural Environment Research Council 2017. BGS Photograph P556198.

Sedgwick's Geological Cross-Section from the Howgill Fells to Baw (Baugh) Fell, crossing the Dent Fault. Transactions of the Geological Society of London, Series 2, Volume 4, 1835.

The fossil fish *Thursius macrolepidotus* (Sedgwick & Murchison) of the Devonian rocks of Caithness, Scotland, discovered and first described by Adam Sedgwick and Roderick Impey Murchison, Transactions of the Geological Society of London, Series 2, Volume 3, 1829. iii

Adam Sedgwick, in 1867, aged 82. Painting by Lowes Cato Dickinson, from J.W. Clark and T.M. Hughes, The Life and Letters of the Reverend Adam Sedgwick, Cambridge University Press, 1890, vol. 2 (Frontispiece) xiv

Map of Dentdale. Drawing by Edward Gower. 7

Sedgwick's birthplace, The Old Parsonage, Dent, as it is today. Photo by John Forder. 10

Sedgwick's house in Norwich. 10

Dent village and the Sedgwick Memorial. Photo by John Forder. 16

Dent Church. Photo by John Forder. 30

Sedbergh School as it was in 1800. Photo by John Forder. 37

Dawson's Rock, Garsdale. Drawing by Edward Gower. 40

John Dawson of Garsdale. From a water colour drawing by William Westoll, 1817. Wellcome Library Image L0005181. 44

Trinity College, Cambridge, from a painting by R.B. Harradan, dated 1845.	**53**
Plate 4 from Sedgwick's 1829 paper on the Magnesian Limestone. Transactions of the Geological Society of London, Series 2, Volume 3, 1829.	**66**
Sir Roderick Impey Murchison (1792-1871). Mezzotint by William Walker, 1851, after W. H. Pickersgill, 1849. Wellcome Library Image V0004176.	**69**
Adam Sedgwick, aged 47. Mezzotint by S. Cousins, 1833, after T. Phillips, 1832. Wellcome Library Image V0005348.	**72**
Plate 50 from Sedgwick's and Murchison's (1840) classic paper on the physical structure of Devonshire. Transactions of the Geological Society of London, Series 2, Volume 5, 1840.	**76**
Title page of Murchison's *magnum opus*, 1839.	**77**
Letter from Sedgwick to Murchison seeking help for the Astronomer Royal and complaining of his health. Source, Geological Society of London.	**90**
Charles Darwin (1809-1882), aged 40. Portrait by T. H. Maguire, 1849.	**101**
Prince Albert, Consort of Queen Victoria (1819-1861). Copyright National Portrait Gallery.	**113**
Cowgill Chapel. Photo by John Forder.	**127**
Adam Sedgwick in later life. Wellcome Library Image V0027136ER	**135**
Back Cover: Sedgwick Memorial, Dent. Photo Colin Speakman.	
Adam Sedgwick. Lithograph by J. H. Lynch after S. Laurence, 1844. Wellcome Library Image V0005349	

Acknowledgements

Without the help of two distinguished historians and scholars, Dr Arthur Raistrick, of Linton, Wharfedale, and Dr Roy Porter, of the Wellcome Institute for the History of Medicine, London, this book could not have been written. Both have been an inspiration and have suggested many new paths to pursue; Dr Porter's detailed and constructive criticism of the manuscript was invaluable. Needless to say any mistakes or misinterpretations that remain are entirely my own. I must also thank Dr Colin Forbes, of the Sedgwick Museum Cambridge, Dr J. B. Morrell, of Bradford University, and Mr D. F. James, of the Cumbria County Archives Department, for their advice and practical help; Miss Mary Barker, who typed the manuscript and whose skill in interpreting my handwriting was heroic; my editor and publisher Mr Tony Harvey, whose enthusiasm and expertise has turned the book into reality; and The Geological Society of London and Trinity College, Cambridge, whose support for the work of someone who is neither a geologist nor a historian in any formal sense, has been truly generous.

This new edition of *Adam Sedgwick – Geologist and Dalesman* would not have been possible without the support of the Yorkshire Geological Society and valued contributions by three of its leading officers – President Andrew Howard, Vice-President John Knight and Treasurer John Holt. To see the book back in print almost 36 years after its first publication is a rare honour and privilege.

Colin Speakman, January 2018

Adam Sedgwick in 1867

1

The granite fountain

In the cobbled main street of the old township of Dent, an isolated village in the north west of the Yorkshire Dales, stands a huge slab of greyish-pink Shap granite with a small drinking fountain built into its base. Inscribed on the stone in crude but powerful Gothic script is

ADAM
SEDGWICK
1785–1873

The starkness, simplicity and power of this monument have few parallels anywhere in the United Kingdom. Its existence challenges the modern visitor to consider who Adam Sedgwick was, and why such a monument should have been erected.

The Dales historian, Dr Arthur Raistrick, has perhaps given a clue to the significance of this monument, which was placed there by a Dales community:

> The whole monument is a moving and dramatic gesture by a people who rarely show their emotions, who fear and distrust high-flown speech and polished phrases, and who give their allegiance to things which endure. In effect they say only what is perfectly true—that their fellow Dalesman, Adam Sedgwick is great enough to need no exposition of his greatness; his name lives among all generations.   (Raistrick, 1950)

Clearly, such a response from hard-headed Dalesmen suggests a remarkable personality, a personality which, as Dr Raistrick implies, has been given a permanent and fitting symbol in that granite fountain:

> The sturdy granite is the true symbol of Sedgwick's character and its association with the spring of water so vital in the life of the village, is as

truly symbolic of Sedgwick's constant intimate fellowship and care for the richer life of the dalesfolk, as is the granite a symbol of his inflexible integrity.   (Raistrick, 1950: 22)

There can be little doubt of Sedgwick's profound and enduring contribution to the life of his own Dale. Although he lived away from Yorkshire for most of his long and distinguished career, Sedgwick never lost contact with his own family and boyhood community, and remained a generous benefactor to that community and to its individuals. In his extreme old age he produced, almost by accident, the remarkable *Memorial by the Trustees of Cowgill Chapel*, which, with its subsequent *Supplement*, has provided modern historians of the Yorkshire Dales with perhaps the most vivid and stimulating account of life in the Dales in the late eighteenth and early nineteenth centuries, the period of Sedgwick's boyhood.

However, what may be a major achievement on the small stage of Dentdale, may, in a national, or even more so in an international context, dwindle to parochial insignificance. A local boy who becomes a Professor in one of the country's greatest universities is regarded, quite naturally, as someone of some importance by the village that produced him. The real question is whether these qualities which elicited such a response in a remote dale have a more universal significance.

Adam Sedgwick had the good fortune to be a geologist during the first half of the nineteenth century which is the period now described as the 'Heroic Age' of Geology when this most empirical of sciences was shaping our entire conception, not only of the structure of our planet, but of man's place within the universe. If for no other reason, his brilliant work unravelling the hitherto incomprehensible ancient rock systems, which were eventually to be known throughout the world as Devonian and Cambrian, would establish Sedgwick as a figure of considerable significance.

There is an especial difficulty in evaluating the achievement of a scientist; unlike his colleagues in artistic fields of creation, the painter, the novelist, the poet, a scientific creator in whatever field must, to some extent, lose his identity in the great flow of ideas that make up a particular scientific discipline. Every scientist builds on the work of his predecessor. Scientific thought develops along a pattern of small and sometimes hardly perceptible accretives—viewpoints change. New generations of geologists since Sedgwick have refined and developed geological concepts to a point which often has made it unnecessary to return to the original sources of investigation. The objectivity of science eliminates the need for individual perception. Unlike the students who return to Wordsworth's *Prelude*, Dickens' *Bleak House* or Turner's last great enigmatic canvases, few but historians of science or geologists re-examining particular regions have found it necessary to re-read the great papers of early geologists.

This is a pity, because these early workers were remarkable personalities, and insight into the methods they used and the perceptions they brought to problems of startling complexity, can still teach us a great deal about the men themselves, the problems they were dealing with and the times in which they lived, and ultimately about ourselves. Sedgwick's own work certainly gives a tangible idea of his achievement as an empirical scientist.

However, there are other aspects of Adam Sedgwick worthy of exploration. His fame as a teacher and lecturer suggests that he had a personal charisma which we can only guess at from numerous independent reports. Yet his was a complex and difficult personality. His directness, bluntness and refusal to compromise could be both a symbol of total integrity and of mulish stubbornness. It could give him immense admiration and almost equally intense dislike.

He had a great gift of communicating with ordinary country or working people and with children, and was not afraid of upsetting the academic Establishment. His bitter and protracted dispute with his former colleague, Sir Roderick Murchison (1792–1871), led to his work being deliberately undervalued by later apologists of Murchison, such as the influential Archibald Geikie (1835–1924).

Most perplexing of all was his chronic inability to produce a sustained geological text, an equivalent of Lyell's *Principles of Geology* or Murchison's *Silurian System*; a brilliant and self-publicizing major work that would have become a standard student text-book. Paradoxically, Sedgwick had a vivid literary style and an ability to use metaphor with stunning force and clarity, qualities that made his lectures famous. His failure to produce a glittering opus on a sufficiently grand scale has resulted in his achievement being eclipsed by gifted rivals. Sedgwick's greatest scientific work consists of a series of magnificent short papers, rather than a single text symbolizing his contributions to scientific thought.

Only relatively recently, among historians of science in both the United Kingdom and in the United States, has a more sophisticated approach to the growth of the scientific imagination in the eighteenth and nineteenth centuries allowed us to see Adam Sedgwick as something more than a kind of gifted primitive; the uncouth churchman who wrong-headedly attacked Charles Darwin (1809–1882); a clumsy, slightly comic rhetorician whom everyone loved, but considered a delightful anachronism. Sedgwick's old-fashioned brand of liberal humanism, his Broad Church Christianity and Natural Theology seems distinctly more attractive to a generation now more keenly aware of the social and moral responsibility of the scientist. His influence on the University of Cambridge and on the teaching of geology, is now more clearly understood.

The purpose therefore, of this short study, is to try to see Adam Sedgwick in this new context. Inevitably it is heavily indebted to the huge and detailed *Life and Letters of Adam Sedgwick* published in 1890, by the zoologist John Willis Clark (1833–1910) and his successor as Woodwardian Professor at Cambridge, Professor Thomas McKenny Hughes (1833–1917). The very massiveness of *The Life and Letters* is a barrier to an objective understanding of Sedgwick; whilst being a magnificent piece of Victorian scholarship, it remains something of a hagiograph; its detail rather obscures the stubborn, reactionary, lonely hypochondriac that Sedgwick became in his later years. New material available since the time of Hughes and Clark, together with unpublished Sedgwick manuscripts in Cambridge, Kendal and elsewhere, have helped fill out the picture and magnify the achievement, and from the perspective of a century help in establishing the full significance of a remarkable and truly fascinating human being.

However, my initial interest was, and remains, Sedgwick's Dentdale. The community that nurtured him and to which he gave so much has changed, almost beyond recognition, since Sedgwick's time. Yet enough that is tangible remains, be it in the incomparably beautiful countryside, lonelier now than in Sedgwick's time, or in the Dentdale people who, for all the influx of tourists, exhibit the same rugged qualities of independence, directness and integrity, inherited from the original Viking settlers. In almost every action he took, throughout a long and varied life Adam Sedgwick remained a Dalesman at heart. This fact, more than anything else, is the key to his personality.

When they erected that massive granite fountain, the Dalesmen of Dent were commemorating more than they knew.

2

Adam o' th' Parsons

Dentdale, one cf the most beautiful and intimate of the narrow valleys of the Yorkshire Dales and described by the unsentimental and hard-headed surveyors for the Board of Agriculture of 1794 as 'the picture of terrestrial paradise' (Rennie, Brown and Shirreff, 1794), owes something of its remarkable greenness to the fact that it faces westwards and is protected from the bitter winds of the north and east by some of the highest fells of the Pennines, whilst capturing the mild, westerly rains. From the west, too, came its original settlers, Norsemen, who developed the Dale not in the manner of a series of nucleated settlements as did their Anglian counterparts to the south and east, but by an extended scattering of freeholdings, with only one township of any significance in the entire 10 miles (16 km) Dale, that of Dent itself.

The tradition of freeholders or 'statesmen' is an extremely strong one in Dentdale, the Manor of Dent having been transferred to freeholders under the control of the Twenty Four Sidesmen of Dent in the sixteenth century (Raistrick, 1967). To this very day, it is noticeable how each farm in the Dale contains not only its equal share of good 'bottom' or meadowland, but a narrow strip of enclosed fellland or rough grazing climbing up to the watershed.

The Sidgwick family came into Dentdale in the mid-sixteenth century, when one Thomas Sidgwick purchased two properties in the Dale, Barklands and Gib's Hall. Both properties are situated on the northern ('sunny') side of the Dale. Thomas married a local girl and his son Leonard inherited the property on his father's death in 1588.

Leonard lived to a great age, the property going to his son, another Thomas in 1646 and then to his grandson, Leonard (the tradition of calling sons after grandfathers still has force in Dales families.) On the barn in front of Gib's Hall the initials LS are still just decipherable on a lintel. They are probably the initials of this Leonard Sidgwick who died in 1687.

Leonard had twin elder sons, named Thomas and John. It was John who inherited Gib's Hall and who became the great-grandfather of Adam Sedgwick. It is significant that John found it necessary to supplement the income of the farm by a trade and built up a prosperous tannery business.

John's son Leonard died in infancy, so that the property was inherited by the second son, another Thomas, also a tanner.

Thomas' only son was Richard, born in 1736 at Gib's Hall. It should be noted that this is not the present Gib's Hall, the fine eighteenth century farmhouse visited by the prolific nineteenth-century novelists, essayists and topographers, Mary and William Howitt. Mary used many of her Dentdale experiences for her novel *Hope On, Hope Ever!* (1840), whilst her husband William included reference to Dentdale and its cottage industries in his celebrated *The Rural Life of England* (1838). The original farmhouse where Richard Sidgwick was born is the derelict, but once fine, Jacobean farmhouse situated just to the east of the present Gib's Hall.

Richard was educated at the local village 'grammar' school, which was founded, as were many others during the sixteenth and early seventeenth centuries, to teach the sons of local parishioners rudimentary Latin, plus some writing and reading and perhaps mathematics; with the local parson sometimes having to combine the duties of schoolmaster with those of parish priest. Dent Grammar School was founded and endowed by local statesmen in 1603, and the original schoolhouse still stands in the northwest corner of the churchyard.

When he was 15, he spent some months at the school of his uncle James Sidgwick, at Horton-in-Ribblesdale, some 16 miles away, and on his uncle's advice was sent to Sedbergh School. This school was already enjoying some local fame, particularly under the headship of Dr Wynne Bateman (1746–82), a graduate of Trinity College, Cambridge, and a fine classical scholar and mathematician (Clarke and Weech, 1925). The fact that Thomas Sidgwick was able to send his son to Sedbergh, which included the cost of lodgings (between £7 and £10 per annum) suggests that the family were reasonably prosperous. However, Richard's time at Sedbergh was merely a preparation for Cambridge, and after receiving additional help and coaching from the brilliant young shepherd mathematician, John Dawson of Garsdale (of whom more in due course), he entered St Catharine's Hall (later St Catharine's College) in 1754.

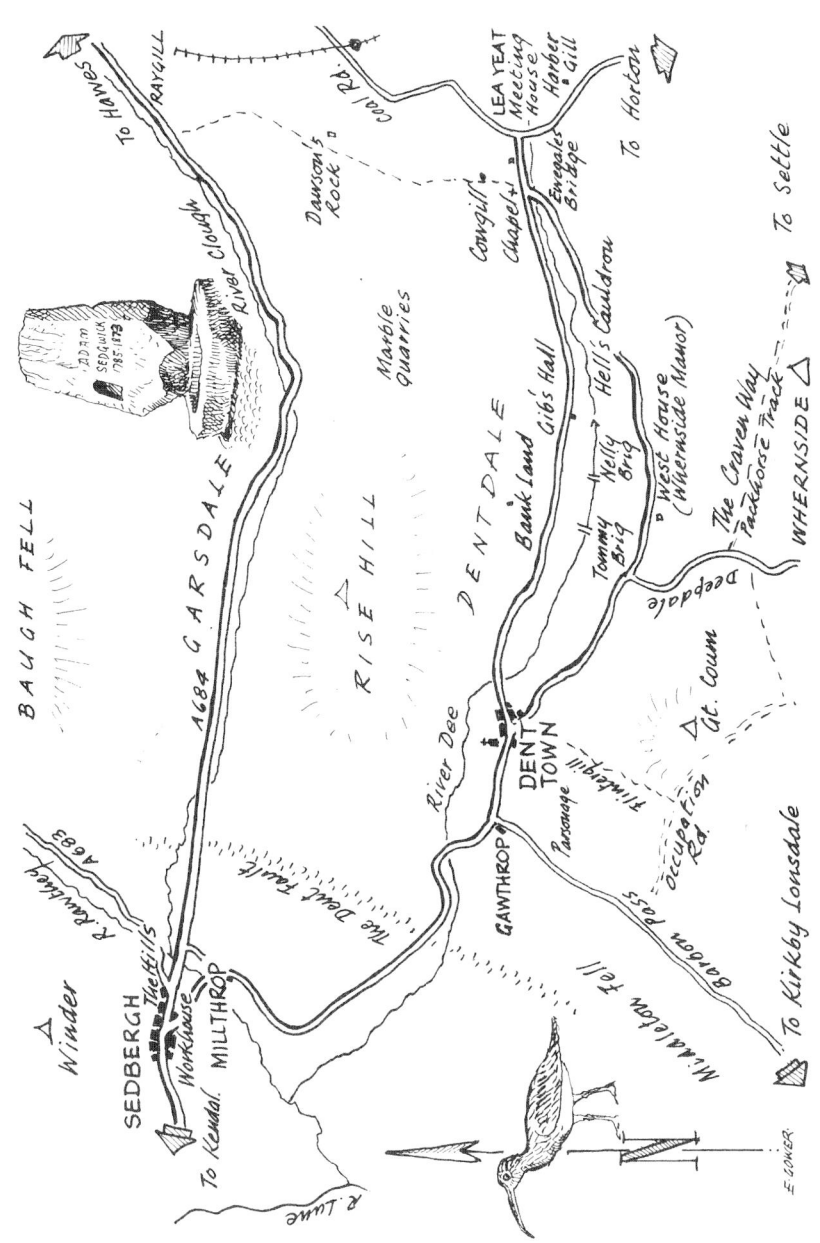

Map of Dentdale

Richard obtained his degree in 1760, was ordained in 1764 and from 1761 to 1768 was curate at Amwell in Hoddesden, Hertfordshire. He married in 1766 the family having about this time changed their surname to the seemingly more acceptable spelling of 'Sedgwick'. In 1768 the living at Dent had become vacant. It was controlled by the 24 'Sidesmen'—all yeoman farmers or statesmen—who decided to present the living to a capable local young man. The fact that it was offered to Richard is sufficient indication of the respect held by the Sedgwick family among the local community, and it also indicates an important facet of that special relationship between cloth and local community that the Sedgwick family shared, i.e. the patronage of the living was held by ordinary members of the community, rather than by a remote aristocratic family. Further, it reflects the especial warmth and respect given to Richard Sedgwick by the villagers. He was 'their' man in every sense.

However, in that same year, 1768, Richard's wife Catherine died in childbirth. The child survived, but she too died in her ninth year. Richard was married soon afterwards to one Margaret Sturgis. This marriage produced seven children, Margaret (1782), Thomas (1783), Adam (1785), Isabel (1787), Ann (1789), John (1791) and Jane (1794). Such a large family meant that Richard's stipend would have been scarcely adequate to feed and clothe them and, therefore, whilst they could not be described as having existed in a state of poverty, the family would certainly not have been affluent, not even by the standards of an eighteenth-century country parson.

Adam was born, on the 22nd March 1785, at the Old Parsonage in Dent. The house still exists, although considerably altered, alongside the village green. It is now a private house. Curiously enough, it was his father's old mathematics tutor, John Dawson, then practising as a local surgeon in Sedbergh, who delivered the child.

In later years, Sedgwick recalled 'as nearly as I can in his own words' Dawson's account of his birth:

> 'The night was tempestuous, and I had much difficulty in making my way to Dent through the thick snow; and when I got to the old vicarage I found that my difficulties were not over. The moment was critical; and though you seemed anxious to show your face to the world, you were for doing it in a strangely preposterous way.' Here he referred me laughing to an early page of *Tristram Shandy*. 'So I sent,' said he, 'your Father's servant to knock up old Margaret Burton to help me to keep you in order.' She was a celebrated midwife, of firmer nerves than the old mathematician. Between them the work was done, and by hook or by crook, I was ushered into the world at about 2 o'clock, a m on March 22nd 1785. I

Adam o' th' Parsons

was then carried downstairs, in old Margaret's apron, to the little back-parlour, where my Father was sitting in some anxiety, as he had been told that his youthful son was beginning life badly and not likely to take good ways. Margaret threw back the corners of her apron and cried out, 'Give you joy sir, give you joy! a fine boy, sir, as like you sir, as one pea is to another.' My Father looked earnestly at me for a moment or two, kissed me, and then turning to the old midwife exclaimed: 'Like me do you say Margaret, why he is as black as a toad!' 'Oh sir, don't speak ill of your own flesh and blood, if I have any eyes in my head he is as white as a lily,' she replied, much shocked, while old Mr Dawson shook his sides, as much, I dare say, as he did when he told me the story. (Clark and Hughes, 1890, vol. I: 45–6)

In more ways than one John Dawson was to prove a remarkable influence on Sedgwick's life.

There seems little reason to doubt Sedgwick when he claimed, in later years, that he had a happy childhood. Like his contemporary, and later acquaintance, Wordsworth, he enjoyed the benefit of a beautiful environment and a good deal of freedom. He also enjoyed an unusually happy family life. As he recalled in later years:

from the old home of my childhood, I can look down the valley and see blue in the distance the crests of the lake mountains which rear their heads over the top of Windermere. All around me is endued by the sweet remembrances of early life, for here I spent my childhood and early boyhood, when my father and mother and three sisters and three brothers were all living in this old home. Our home was humble, but we were a merry crew, rich in health and rich in brotherly love. (Clark and Hughes, 1890, vol. I: 53)

In my early days we all dined together. Parson and his wife and the schoolmaster, and seven children and the two servant lasses. The lasses served the plates to us, and then they sat down with us. But when we grew up a little this primitive arrangement was changed. (Sedgwick, 1862)

Like his father, Adam attended the local school where Mr Parker, his godfather, was schoolmaster. The child seems to have been a reasonably lively scholar, even though as an infant 'given to tearing books rather than reading them' (Clark and Hughes, 1890, vol. I: 47).

He was taught by his father after the departure of Mr Parker in 1794, and soon gained a reputation among the villagers as a bright, dependable boy, known with characteristic terseness as 'Adam o' th' Parsons', and frequently entrusted with important errands or messages. He was a strong and energetic lad, exploring the local country-

Adam Sedgwick

Above Sedgwick's birthplace, The Old Parsonage, Dent, as it is today. *Below* Sedgwick's house in Norwich.

side, rambling on the fells, fishing the becks, and even borrowing a gun for a bit of rough shooting.

Albeit with a certain amount of professional hindsight, he later claimed that his boyhood wanderings helped establish the habits of observation that made the later geologist:

One of my early employments on a half holiday in Dent woods was as I well remember, noting the conspicuous fossils of the mountain limestone in each side of the valley. It was not until years after that I understood its structure, but these early rambles no doubt aided to establish a taste for out-of-doors observation. (Clark and Hughes, 1890, vol. I: 50)

Two people were particularly powerful influences on Sedgwick during his childhood. The first, not surprisingly, was his father. Richard Sedgwick was a scholar. It is clear much of the son's ambition was derived from an admiration of his father's ability and drive, and his father's success in making the leap from being the son of a local tradesman to entering the professional classes through the avenue most easily available to a boy from relatively humble origins—the clergy. But it was more than this. It was an admiration of the genuine respect which Richard Sedgwick had gained from the local community. It was with a sense of quite extraordinary pride that the boy could observe the bond of affection between parishioners and priest evident every Sunday morning.

When in my childhood I saw, on a Sunday morning, the ample convexity of my Father's well-dressed and well-powdered wig, I thought it one of the most beautiful sights in the world. I remember too, as he went, with his usual light step, towards the Church, and saluted his friends who were come to join in the sacred services of the day, that each head was uncovered as he passed. It was not any token of unmanly servility; but it belonged to the manners of the times: and it was, I think, also connected with an aristocratic feeling, which modified the thoughts and manners and dress of the older Statesmen. They loved my Father, because by birth he was one of themselves, and because of his kindness and purity of life. They were proud of him too, because he was a graduate of the University of Cambridge, and had been living in good literary society some years before he fixed his home in Dent. Part of his influence arose, also, from the reputation of his skill in athletic exercises; and from a principle of action which he carried out through his long life—never to allow his conception of his sacred duties to come, on questions of moral indifference, into a rude collision with the habits and prejudices of the valley. The consequence was that he held an almost unbounded influence over his Flock. (Sedgwick, 1868: 64–5)

This 'skill in athletic exercises' reflected an interest in outdoor sport and recreation which was hardly typical of the habits of mind of most eighteenth-century clergymen:

My old Father (he was about 50 years old when I was born) was a very happy cheerful man. He did many things that would now seem strange, if done by a clergyman. He encouraged field sports. He rather liked a good football match on a Sunday evening. Of course he did not go to see it: but he used to say 'the lads come from a distance and only meet once a week. Far better they should be merry and happy in the field than in the public house.' And one or two men who were famous in the football matches used to come to the Parsonage on the Sunday evenings, after the game was over, to attend the family prayers. They were not aware of any incongruity in so doing. (Sedgwick, 1862)

This involvement in village sports, is a clear indication of the involvement in the local community practised by Richard Sedgwick. Inter-village contests which included 'leaping, foot-racing and wrestling' as well as football could be riotous occasions when 'the spirit of parochial rivalry sometimes, however, lead to mischief; and in some cases the games were carried on with a savage energy'. But Richard Sedgwick had that kind of authority which could control such a situation with an astonishing ease:

I remember an occasion, in my very early life, when one of the old Statesmen, John Mason of Schoolbred, came in great haste and out of breath into the Vicarage, and wished to see my Father. 'I hope you will kindly come and help us' he said 'or there will be mischief at the meeting of fieldsports in the Great Holm. At a late parochial meeting there was a sad accident, which led to mutual charges of foul dealing. Several of us have been asking them to pledge their word, as true men, that all shall be done fairly and kindly: but their blood is up and they refused with scorn, till one of the men cried out. 'We will play fairly if Mr Sedgwick will come and be the umpire of the foot-ball match.' 'I will go with all my heart,' said my Father, 'that I may be a peace-maker; and I should like to see the game. Come, Adam, take my hand, and you shall walk with me to the foot-ball match.' I right willingly obeyed the order: and though more than 80 years have passed away since that day, yet I remember standing on the high embankment by the river-side, and my father's figure at this moment seems to be living before my mind's eye. I remember his cheerful countenance, beaming with kindness and lighted by the flush of health; his broad-brimmed hat, looped at the sides in a way that told of a former fashion; his full-bottomed wig, well dressed and powdered; and his large silver shoe-buckles; all of them objects of my childish admiration. But what I wish most to notice was the respectful manner of the crowd. Many of them came to thank my father, and each one spoke with uncovered head. Harmony and good-will were restored to the excited combatants, and the great foot-ball match went on and ended in joyful temper and mutual good-will. I have no remembrance which party it was that carried off the prize of victory. (Sedgwick, 1870: 42)

It was this brand of tolerant, pragmatic Christianity which so influenced Adam Sedgwick; liberal, compassionate, humane yet able to assert the required degree of authority when required. Richard Sedgwick's well-known detestation of slavery, a passion inherited by his son, was based on more than a theological aversion. Barely a mile from the Parsonage, the Sills, a local family with considerable landowning and plantation interests in Jamaica, brought Jamaican slaves back to Dentdale to build a colonial-style mansion at West House, where their ill-treatment became a considerable local scandal. (Lyon, 1978)

However, Richard Sedgwick was also a scholar; when his old friend John Dawson walked over from Sedbergh, a period of lively, intellectual discussion would follow.

In particular, Richard Sedgwick mourned the forces at work which were bringing about the catastrophic decline of the community in which he served.

> He well knew the habits and character of his countrymen; and he lived among them like a brother, and was much loved by them. Many a time have I heard him describe and lament that downward movement and social decay of his native valley, against which it seemed almost in vain to struggle. (Sedgwick, 1868: x–xi)

Richard Sedgwick lived to a great age, retiring to Flintergill, above Dent, and dying in his 93rd year. In his later years he lost his sight, and though he had a Curate, would still occasionally take a service from memory, most particularly the Burial Service which, according to witnesses, was a remarkably moving experience.

The other major influence on Adam stemmed from his sister Isabella, who was less than two years his junior. It would seem that Adam and Isabella were extremely close. As he later recalled:

> She was my never-failing companion; and I taught her, in our wild valley of Dent, all sorts of boy's tricks. For example she would run like a monkey up a tree to peep into a magpie's nest. The effect of this training gave her excellent, robust health and it matured her sweet natural temper—and when she grew up she was a mild, gently feminine, unselfish person, beloved by everyone. (Clark and Hughes, 1890, vol. I: 54)

Her tragically early death, at the age of 36 in 1823, left a searing scar on Sedgwick for the rest of his days. As he wrote in 1849:

> I once lost a sister, the dearest of all my sisters, and the darling companion of my early years. She was a woman of most placid temper, yet of great personal courage. We had our little squabbles about our toys when we were children; but after we reached our teens, I think I never heard so much as a word from her lips that was not spoken in kindness. Her death was a grievous blow to me, and I never visit my native hills without being reminded of her at every turn. (Clark and Hughes, 1890, vol. I: 54)

The day after Isabella's death, Sedgwick's youngest sister, Jane, gave birth a few days prematurely to a daughter, doubtless as a result of the emotional shock, who was christened Margaret Isabella. Sedgwick always had a peculiar fondness for this niece even calling her his own child, 'quite as dear as a daughter'. In spite of the difference in years, a deep bond developed between them as she grew up. He never married, and she was his constant companion and his nurse in his old age and infirmity.

As Sedgwick grew older, he particularly enjoyed the companionship of young women, treating them with a tenderness and consideration not all that common among elderly bachelors, particularly those of an academic persuasion. Many of his most characteristically generous and lively letters were to his nieces or other young ladies of his acquaintance, and it is not too fanciful to suggest that the remarkable bond between the two Isabellas of his life influenced this.

3

The Statesmen of Dent

In his later years, through letters, in conversation, and above all through the magnificent *Memorial*, Adam Sedgwick has left a remarkable record of Dentdale and its community as it was at the time of his boyhood, that is the end of the eighteenth and the turn of the nineteenth centuries.

His memory, at the end of his life, retained an unusual clarity and sharpness. At that age of 85 he could still recall 'to the farthest boundary within my memory' events of '82 or 83' years previously, such as, for example, when as an infant in his nurse's arms, he watched the tower being built on Dent Church, already curious about the engineering techniques employed: 'I saw them elevating large blocks of stone by the help of Triangles, known in Dent by the name of Teagles.' (Sedgwick, 1870: 36).

Or again, a little later, at an event of considerable importance to Dent, the public opening of the belfry of the church, 'a day of great rejoicing in the Dale', he was carried by a local youth for a closer look at the great bells, an experience for the child which was not entirely pleasurable:

> A young man, named Thomas Batty, took me from the nurse's arms, and carried me up the ladders of the steeple to shew me the bells while they were ringing their merry peal. However sweet the bells might be at a proper distance, their noise was terrific and enough to tear the bones of the head asunder when the ear was in the same room with them. So I kicked with my little feet against the breast of the bearer, and he soon took me down and restored me to my nurse's arms. It was the same man who eight or ten years afterwards filled the office of constable. (Sedgwick, 1870: 36).

The church bells had a significance for the community which is diffi-

Dent village and the Sedgwick Memorial.

cult for us to now recognize. As well as expressing a communal awareness of the constant pattern of individual human joy or tragedy, birth, marriage and death, they also had a part to play in the participation, by the village, in great events on the world stage far beyond the valley. Nelson's victories at Cape St Vincent or the Nile, for example, brought forth peals of jubilation.

Nowhere is this better illustrated than the account of how Sedgwick himself brought to Dent the news of Wellington's great victory at Waterloo. It was in the Spring of 1815, when the University had gone down early owing to a typhoid epidemic in Cambridge, and Sedgwick had returned to the safety of his family in Dent. Rumour of impending victory or disaster was rife, and the sound of Sedbergh bells made him realise news was at hand.

> It was a year of great events in the history of Christendom, and the fate of Europe seemed once more to be hanging upon the issue of a battle. At that time we had a post three days a week, and each of those days, to the great comfort of the aged Postman, I rode over to Sedbergh to bring back

the newspapers and the letters to my countrymen. Gloomy reports had reached us of a battle and a retreat; but another and greater battle was at hand: and on one of my anxious journeys, just as I past over the Riggs, I heard the sound of the Sedbergh bells. Could it be, I said, the news of a victory? No! it was a full hour before the time of the Postman's arrival. A minute afterwards I saw a countryman returning hastily from Sedbergh. 'Pray what means that ringing?' I said, 'News, Sir, sich as niver was heard before: I kña lile about it; but the Kendal Postman had just come an hour before his time. He was all covered with ribbons, and his horse was all covered with froth.' Hearing this, I spurred my horse to the Kendal Postman's speed; and it was my joyful fortune to reach Sedbergh, not many minutes after the arrival of the Gazette Extraordinary which told us of the great victory of Waterloo. After joining in the cheers and gratulations of my friends at Sedbergh, I returned to Dent with what speed I could: and such was the anxiety of the day that many scores of my brother Dalesmen met me on the way: and no time was lost in our return to the market-place of Dent. They ran by my side as I urged my horse: and then mounting on the great blocks of black marble, from the top of which my countrymen have so often heard the voice of the auctioneer and the town-crier, I read, at the highest pitch of my voice, the news from the Gazette Extraordinary to the anxious crowd which pressed round me. After the tumultuous cheers had somewhat subsided, I said, 'Let us thank God for this great victory, and let the six bells give us a merry peal.' As I spoke these words an old weather-beaten soldier who stood under me said, 'It is great news, and it is good news, if it brings us peace. Yes,' continued the old soldier, 'let the six bells ring merrily; but it has been a fearful struggle; and how many aching hearts will there be when the list of killed and wounded becomes known to the mothers, wives and daughters of those who fought and bled for us! But the news is good, and let the six bells ring merrily.'   (Sedgwick, 1870: 38–9)

News, in 1815, travelled only as fast as a man could travel on foot or horseback; yet it was essentially a public occasion, a shared experience in a way that is now no longer possible. For that reason, the fact that the bells were, by the 1860s, silent was, to Sedgwick, a reflection on the decline of a community which in turn, suggested an almost moral decay:

On all these great occasions I was an eye-witness and a partaker of the rejoicings and excitement in my native Dale. But how does all this tell upon the objects of this Supplement? Not much upon the condition of the Dale; but much upon the feelings of the people. The belfry was first opened on an occasion of public joy in which young and old were the sharers; and for many a long year my brother Dalesmen were proud of their six bells, and rejoiced in the liberality of those who had lived before them. But a strange change had, since those days, come, for a while, over the inhabitants of Dent. For, about two or three years since, when I revis-

> ited the home of my early life, the bells were as silent as the grave; because the inhabitants grudged the little fee which in former times had been paid to the ringers. In my younger days, sooner than have believed this, I should almost have thought that the bells would have sounded of themselves by the might of sympathy with the people's hearts. But time, that changes all things, has in some things greatly changed the hearts of my countrymen.   (Sedgwick, 1870: 39)

What was the cause of this decline? The reasons were, of course, primarily, economic. The effects of the Industrial Revolution were as profound, if a good deal less obvious, on the self-sufficient rural community of Dent, as they were on the booming new industrial areas of the West Riding and South Lancashire, with their factories, pollution and soul-destroying slums.

In 1800, Dentdale's economy was sustained by a pattern of mixed farming undertaken by small freeholders or statesmen that had not, in essence, changed since medieval times. Mary Howitt, (1799–1888), in the opening chapter of her novel *Hope On, Hope Ever!*, gives a graphic, and probably fairly accurate account of the self-sufficient world of the Dentdale statesmen at this period:

> the good people of Dentdale form a little world in themselves. Each is generally the proprietor of his own small section of the hill-side—that is, between rivulet and rivulet—which form the natural landmarks of each demesne. Two or three fields, called 'pasture-heads' are generally enclosed and cultivated near the house, where oats, wheat, and potatoes are grown for family consumption; and the lower descent of the hill, down to the level of the valley, is used for grass and hay for the horses and cows; but the upper parts, called 'the fell-side', are grazed by large flocks of sheep, geese, and wild ponies. Sheep, however, form the wealth of the valley; and the sheep-washings and shearings made as blithe holidays as the harvest-homes, and the wakes and fairs, of other district.
>
> (M. Howitt, 1840)

The income from farming was augmented by a thriving cottage industry, the knitting of garments from local wool, particularly stockings, hats and gloves. Sedgwick describes the development of the industry:

> Wool must have been a great staple produce of the valley from its earliest history. The greater part of it was exported: but some of it was retained for domestic use; then worked into form by hand-cards of antique fashion (which, in my childhood, I have seen in actual use); and then spun into a very coarse and clumsy thread; and so it supplied the material for a kind of rude manufacture, that went, I think, under the elegant name of Bump.
>
> But as art advanced, our Dalesmen gradually became familiar with the

The Statesmen of Dent

> fine material prepared by the wool-comber: and before the beginning of last century, Dent became known for its manufacture and export of yarn-stockings of the finest quality. Some of the more active and long sighted Statesmen of the Dales, taking upon themselves the part of middle-men between manufacturers and the consumers, used occasionally to mount their horses, and ride up to London to deal personally with the merchants of Cheapside, and to keep alive the current of rural industry.
>
> At a further stage in the industry of our countrymen, worsted, that had been spun by machinery, came into common use; and the knit worsted-stockings were the great articles of export from the Northern Dales. Such became the importance of this export, about the middle of the last century, that Government Agents were placed at Kirkby Lonsdale, Kendal and Kirkby Stephen, during 'the seven years' war,' for the express purpose of the securing for the use of the English army (then in service on the Continent) the worsted stockings knit by the hands of the Dalesmen; and in this trade Dent had an ample share. (Sedgwick, 1868: 58)

Kendal was the focal point of this thriving trade; Dr Raistrick notes that in the later eighteenth century around 5,000 people in the Kendal area were employed in fine-stocking knitting. There were over 120 wool combers, each of whom could keep five spinners employed, each spinner supplying yarn for four or five knitters (Raistrick, 1968: 118–19)

Most of the manufactured material would be taken into Kendal market each week by packpony train. A gang of 20 packhorses came to Kendal each week from Sedbergh, Kirkby Lonsdale, Orton, Dent and other neighbouring villages, and in 1801 it is recorded that an average of 840 pairs of knitted stockings came from Sedbergh and Dent.

> The hosiers used regularly to attend the markets of all the towns, at stated times all the villages and hamlets within 20 miles of the circumjacent country, to give out worsted which they carried with them for the purpose, and take in the stockings that had been knit during the interval between each visit. (C. Nicholson, 1861: 241)

The actual knitting was done in upstairs workshops or galleries in some of the older houses, by men and children whilst tending cattle or sheep, and on winter evenings or at social gatherings. Sedgwick gives a remarkable account of a Dentdale 'Sitting', when the wives of Dent would gather together to work and talk, or even share in a reading from some familiar literary classic.

> While speaking of the habits and manner of my countrywomen, I may remark that their industry had then a social character. Their machinery and the material of their fabrics they constantly bore about with them.

Hence the knitters of Dent had a reputation of being lively gossips; and they worked together in little clusters—not in din and confinement like that of a modern manufactory—but each one following the leading of her fancy; whether among her friends, or rambling in the sweet scenery of the valley; and they were notable for their thrifty skill as for their industry. And speaking of both sexes, the manners of our countrymen may have been thought rude and unpolished from lack of commerce with the world; and their prosperity in a former century may sometimes have roused the envy and the jests and satire of those who were less handy than themselves; but for many a long year theirs was the winning side.

Their social habits led them to form little groups of family parties, who assembled together, in rotation, round one blazing fire, during the winter evenings. This was called *ganging a sitting* to a neighbour's house: and the custom prevailed, though with diminished frequency, during the early years I spent in Dent. Let me try to give a picture of one of these scenes in which I have myself been, not an actor but a looker on. A *Statesman's* house in Dent had seldom more than two floors, and the upper floor did not extend to the wall where was the chief fireplace, but was wainscoted off from it. The consequence was, that a part of the ground floor, near the fire-place, was open to the rafters; which formed a wide pyramidal space, terminating in the principal chimney of the house. It was in this space, chiefly under the open rafters, that the families assembled in the evening. Though something rude to look at, the space gave the advantage of a good ventilation. About the end of the seventeenth century grates and regular flues began to be erected; but during Dent's greatest prosperity, they formed the exception and not the rule.

Let me next shortly describe the furniture of this space where they held their evening '*Sittings*'. First there was a blazing fire in a recess of the wall; which in early times was composed of turf and great logs of wood. From one side of the fireplace ran a bench, with a strong and sometimes ornamentally carved back, called a *lang settle*. On the other side of the fire-place was the Patriarch's wooden and well carved arm-chair; and near the chair was the *sconce* adorned with crockery. Not far off was commonly seen a well-carved cupboard, or cabinet, marked with some date that fell within a period of fifty years after the restoration of Charles the Second; and fixed to the beams of the upper floor was a row of cupboards, called the *Cat-malison* (the cat's curse); because from its position it was secure from poor grimalkin's paw. One or two small tables, together with chairs or benches, gave seats to all the party there assembled. Rude though the room appeared, there was in it no sign of want. It had many signs of rural comfort: for under the rafters were suspended bunches of herbs for cookery, hams sometimes for export, flitches of bacon, legs of beef, and other articles salted for domestic use.

They took their seats; and then began the work of the evening; and with a speed that cheated the eye they went on with their respective tasks. Beautiful gloves were thrown off complete; and worsted stockings made

The Statesmen of Dent

good progress. There was no dreary noise of machinery; but there was the merry heart-cheering sound of the human tongue. No one could foretell the current of the evening's talk. They had their ghost tales; and their love tales; and their battles of jests and riddles; and their ancient songs of enormous length, yet heard by ears that were never weary. Each in turn was to play its part according to the humour of the *Sitting*. Or by way of change, some lassie who was bright and *renable* was asked to read for the amusement of the party. She would sit down; and, apparently without interrupting her work by more than a single stitch, would begin to read—for example, a chapter of *Robinson Crusoe*. In a moment the confusion of sounds ceased: and no sound was heard but the reader's voice, and the click of the knitting needles, while she herself went on knitting: and she would turn over the leaves before her (as a lady does those of her music-book from the stool of her piano), hardly losing a second at such successive leaf, till the chapter was done. Or at another and graver party, some one, perhaps, would read a chapter from the *Pilgrims Progress*. It also charmed all tongues to silence: but, as certainly, led to a grave discussion so soon as the reading ceased.

I am not drawing from my imagination, but from the memory of what I have seen and heard in my younger, school-boy days; and I only knew Dent while in its decline. Such were the happy family *Sittings* in which labour and sorrow were divorced, and labour and joy were for a while united.   (Sedgwick, 1868).

However, the prosperity of Dentdale was not confined to farming and knitting. The Dale was known for its Galloway ponies, for its manufacture of butter, salted in casks and firkins manufactured in the Dale by thriving coopers. Dentdale had its own cornmills, and its own quarries, producing not only good quality sandstones for building and limestone with its many uses, but the spectacular Dent 'Black' marbles a form of limestone highly prized in the nineteenth century because of its many ornamental uses. There were even supplies of coal, worked from small pits on the ancient track between Garsdale and Dentdale (still known as 'The Coal Road'), or by an enterprise that well reveals the energy and determination of the old statesmen to wrest a living from the resources that were available.

Early, I believe, in the last century a small *Statesman* called Buttermere found the bed of coal under the *upper Limestone* of the Town Fell; just under the last rise of the Crag. The bed appeared at first sight too thin to be worked for profit; but on examination it proved to be free from sulphur, and well fitted for the works of the whitesmiths in Kendal. He therefore engaged the help of the country miners, and carried on his work for years conveying to Kendal, by a train of pack-horses (seventeen miles over the mountains), the coal which he drew from a bed not more than six or seven inches thick. And, spite of the smallness of his produce, and the cost of its primitive mode of transport, he went on till he had realised a fortune—not small, according to the humble standard of his countrymen—and he ended as a public benefactor to his Valley.

A tale like this does impressively tell us of the vast changes that were wrought during the dealings of the last century. Joseph Buttermere's coal, as a matter of export, would now be scouted as a mere worthless mockery. Yet I think the tale deserves notice as a curious record of one of the primitive modes in which our old *Statesmen* dealt with those who, to them, were in a kind of outer world. (Sedgwick, 1868: 60–1)

Almost everything that the community required was manufactured by the craftsmen of the valley; there was a sufficient surplus from the rewards of the cottage industry to generate at least a limited amount of wealth, and the market at Kendal in the west represented the outer world for most inhabitants of the Dale. London, or the great manufacturing centres then appearing in the north of England might as well have been on another planet.

A graphic illustration of this isolation is revealed by the use, at the time of Sedgwick's childhood, of a primitive and archaic cart, built with a fixed wheel and axle, an arrangement which dated from medieval times. Nonetheless, on the narrow and rough lanes of Dentdale, they sufficed, and therefore survived:

> Among the changes and great improvements on Dent, I may mention the public roads, which are now both sound and good. I remember some roads in Dent so narrow that there was barely room for one of the little country carts to pass along them; and they were so little cared for, that, in the language of the country, the way was as 'rough as the beck staens'. I remember too when the carts and the carriages were of the rudest character; moving on wheels which did not revolve about their axle; but the wheels and their axle were so joined as to revolve together. Four strong pegs of wood, fixed in a cross-beam under the cart, embraced the axle-tree; which revolved between the pegs, as the cart was dragged on, with a horrible amount of friction that produced a creaking noise, in the expressive language of the Dales called 'Jyking'. The friction was partially relieved by frequent doses of tar, administered to the pegs from a ram's horn which hung behind the cart. Horrible were the creakings and Jykings which set all teeth on edge while the turf-carts or coal-carts were dragged from the mountains to the houses of the Dalesmen in the Hamlets below. Such were the carts that brought the turf and the coals to the Vicarage, during all the early days of my boyhood. But now there is not a young person in the Valley who perhaps has so much as seen one of these clog-wheels, as they were called: and our power of transport, to be more perfect only wants a better line of road, that might easily be made to avoid those steep inclines, which are now a grievous injury to the traffic of the Valley. (Sedgwick, 1870: 41–2)

During Sedgwick's boyhood the major form of transport was the packhorse train. Green tracks, climbing the most direct and steep routes across the fells, still abound in the Dent region. Adam Sedgwick gives a vivid picture of a statesman and his family making their way not by carriage, but by pack-way, doubtless riding one of the sturdy little 'Galloways' or Scottish pack-ponies:

> But with all our modern advantages of transport, Dent has lost the picturesque effect of its trains of pack-horses and many time, on a Sunday morning, I have regretted that I could no longer see the old Statesman riding along the rough and rugged road, with his wife behind him mounted upon a gorgeous family pillion; and his daughters walking briskly at his side, in their long flowing scarlet cloaks with silken hoods.
> (Sedgwick, 1870: 42)

Wordsworth, writing in 1810 about the eighteenth cenury 'estatesmen' of nearby Westmorland, an area identical in many respects to Dentdale, describes

> a perfect Republic of Shepherds and Agriculturists, among whom the plough of each man as confined to the maintenance of his own family, or to the occasional accommodation of his neighbour. Two or three cows furnished each family with milk or cheese. The chapel was the only edifice that presided over these dwellings, the supreme head of this pure commonwealth; the members of which existed in the midst of a powerful empire like an ideal society or an organized community whose constitution had been imposed and regulated by the mountains which protected it.   (Wordsworth, 1810: 101–2)

One naturally takes Wordsworth's idealized and perhaps romantic view as that of a radical whose burning republicanism was not quite extinguished and who could still see in rural life an echo of Rousseauesque simplicity threatened by industrialization.

Nonetheless, the 'Brotherhood of the Dales' is a phrase which Sedgwick also uses with some significance. If Dentdale was not quite Wordsworth's 'visionary mountain republic', nor the 'land of rural opulence and glee' that Sedgwick supposes (his private nightmare as a Cambridge undergraduate, and College Fellow, was that circumstances might force him to return to Dent to become village parson and schoolmaster), nonetheless the image of a prosperous, stable, democratically organized community, of Low Church inclination, God-fearing, hard-working, and reasonably happy, is a convincing one.

Wordsworth has identified, reasonably accurately, the forces among the estatesmen of Westmorland that led to a catastrophic economic decline:

> About the same time that strangers began to be attracted to the country, and to feel a desire to settle in it, the difficulty that would have stood in the way of procurring situations was lessened by an unfortunate alteration in the circumstances of the native peasantry, proceeding from a cause which then began to operate, and is now felt in every house. The family of each man, whether estatesman or farmer, formerly had two-fold support; first the produce of his lands and flocks; and secondly, the profit drawn from the employment of the women and children, as manufacturers; spinning their own wool in their own homes (work done chiefly in the winter season), and carrying it to market for sale. Hence, however the number of children, the income of the family kept pace with its increase. But, by the invention and universal application of machinery, this second resource has been cut off; the gains being so far reduced as not to be sought but by a few aged persons disabled from other employment. Doubtless, the invention of machinery has not been to those people a pure loss; for the profits arising from home manufacturers operated as a strong temptation to choose that mode of labour in neglect of husbandry. They also participate in the general benefit which the island has derived from the increased value of the produce of land, brought about by the establishment of manufactures, and in the consequent quickening of agricultural industry. But this is far from making them amends; and now that home manufacturers might, at many seasons of the year, employ themselves with advantage in the fields beyond what they are accustomed to do, yet still all possible exertion in this way cannot rationally be expected from persons whose agricultural knowledge is so confined, and above all, where there must necessarily be so small a capital. The consequence then is that proprietors and farmers being no longer able to maintain themselves upon small farms, several are united in one, and the buildings go to decay or are destroyed; and that the lands of the estatesmen being mortgaged, and the owners constrained to part with them, they fall into the hands of wealthy purchasers, who in like manner unite and consolidate; and, if they wish to become residents erect new mansions out of the ruins and the ancient cottages, whose little enclosures, with all mild graces that grew out of them disappear.
>
> (Wordsworth, 1810: 126–7)

Thus as Sedgwick notes:

> Each 'statesman's' home had its garden and its orchard, and other good signs of domestic comfort. But alas with rare exceptions, these goodly tokens have now passed out of sight; or are to be feebly traced by some aged crab-tree or the stump of an old plum-tree which marks the site of the ancient family orchard. (Sedgwick, 1868: vii)

A further factor was the growing wealth of industrial England, outside the Dales. The *nouveau riche* of the Sheffield iron-works, of the Stoke potteries, and of the Lancashire cotton mills, looked to the Lake District and the Yorkshire Dales as suitable county retreats, in which to purchase an estate and perhaps build a mansion. The surplus capital of the new manufacturers meant the doom of the rural and pastoral yeomanry. It meant a gradual transference from owner-occupier to tenants, and absentee landlords: 'A rented farm was once a rare exception to the general rule: but now nearly the whole dale, from end to end, is in the occupation of farmers with very small capital, and living at a high rack-rent.' (Sedgwick, 1868: vii).

At the time Sedgwick was writing this, the population of Dent had declined from a total of 1,773 at the first census of 1801 (by no means the zenith of Dent's prosperity) to around 1,360 and worse was to follow. In 1971 the populaton was a mere 590, less than a third of the 1801 figure. It had once been larger than that of Sedbergh; it is now a quarter of Sedbergh's size.

The gradual decline of Dentdale's economy had many repercussions. Many of the trade and allied 'service' industries which had once given Dent its self-sufficiency, declined and finally disappeared; nor was there the corresponding flood of incomers, as in Wordsworth's Lake District, which, welcome or not, would help sustain a viable local community infrastructure.

To some extent, Sedgwick's *Memorial* is an extended and melancholy hymn of regret for the changes that had overtaken Dent in his own lifetime. The sorrow is mixed with anger, an anger at the absentee landlords who had assisted the decay:

> The whole aspect of the village of Dent has been changed within my memory and some may perhaps think that it has been changed for the better. But I regret the loss of some old trees that covered its nakedness; and most of all the two ancient trees that adorned the Church-yard, and were cut down by hands which had no right to touch twig of them. I regret the loss of the grotesque and rude, but picturesque old galleries, which once gave a character to the streets; and in some parts of them almost shut out the sight of the sky from those who travelled along the pavement. For rude as were the galleries, they once formed a highway of communication to a dense and industrious rural population which lived on flats or single floors. And the galleries that ran before the successive doors, were at all seasons places of free air; and in the summer season were places of mirth and glee, and active, happy industry. For there might be heard the buzz of the spinning-wheel, and the hum and the songs of those who were carrying on the labours of the day; and the merry jests and greetings sent down to those who were passing through the streets. Some of the galleries were gone before the days of my earliest

memory, and all of them were hastening to decay. Not a trace of them is left now. The progress of machinery undermined the profitable industry of Dent, which, in its best days, had no mechanical help beyond the needle, the hand-card, or the cottage spinning-wheel. I still regret the loss within the village streets of those grotesque outward signs of a peculiar industry which was honourable to my countrymen; but has now left hardly a remnant of its former life. I regret its old market-cross, and the stir and bustle of its market days. I regret its signboards dangling across the streets; which though sometimes marking spots of boisterous revelry, were at the same time the tokens of a rural opulence. Most of all do I regret the noble trees which were the pride and ornament of so many of the ancient 'statesmen's' houses throughout the valley. Nearly all the old forest-trees are gone: but the valley is still very beautiful, from the continual growth of young wood which springs up, self-planted, from the gills and hedgerows.

Nearly all the landed property of the five hamlets of Dent has past out of the hands of the ancient stock of native 'statesmen'. Many of them, not having learnt to adapt their habits to the gradual change of times, were ruined, and sank into comparative poverty. Some migrated in search of a better market for their talents A few old families stood the trial, and still possess the freehold of their ancestors, with some additions of their own: and I need not tell my countrymen that there are one or two present examples of landed property in the valley which exceed any that was held by a single 'statesmen' in the days of its greatest prosperity.

But alas, these larger proprietors are no longer among the resident yeomanry of the valley.   (Sedgwick, 1868: vii–xi)

However, the *Memorial* is more than a sentimental regret for what might have been, a perhaps inevitable pattern of change. It is a human document, a record of extraordinary power of a community which even if it was doomed, still had extraordinary vitality. The value of Sedgwick's testimony lies, too, in the fact that he was a member of the community he describes, he writes about it not as the rural sociologist, the outsider, but as someone within that community, who nonetheless was sufficiently detached because of his later training and background, to see it within a wider context. As a member of that community, he was also in touch with folk memory, rumour and gossip, an awareness which extended far back into the mists of the early eighteenth century.

One such quite extraordinary memory was recorded in conversation with W. Aldis Wright, Vice Master of Trinity College, Cambridge, just a fortnight before Sedgwick's death early in 1873. It records a link between Dentdale and Prince Charlie's abortive rebellion of 1745 when the Highlanders retreated through the North of England.

The Statesmen of Dent

> When I was a boy there was living in Dent a certain Matthew Potts whom we lads looked up to as a hero because when he was an apprentice he and another lad had run away from their masters and followed the fortunes of the Scottish army in their retreat Northward. They were witnesses of the battle of Clifton Moor near Penrith, which Scott described in Waverley, and Potts carried off from the battlefield a broadsword, a target, and a tortoise-shell comb stolen from the body of a young Highland Officer. The young scamps lived by milking the cows they found on the moors, and they grew so familiar with the scenes of battle that they boasted of having set a dead Highlander astride of a stone wall with a pebble in his mouth to keep it open.
>
> When the Highlanders marched through Kendal they were very badly shod and laid hands on all the boots and shoes they could find. One of them went into the stables of the King's Arms and appropriated a pair of boots belonging to the ostler, who was out of the way. As the thief was lagging behind his comrades to put on his ill-gotten gains he was overtaken by the owner of the boots a truculent fellow, who ran him through with a pitchfork and killed him on the spot. My father, who was a boy of ten years old at the time knew the ostler well, and had often heard the story. I think the historians record that a soldier in the Duke of Perth's regiment met his death at Kendal, but say nothing of the manner of it.
>
> (Clark and Hughes, 1890, vol. I: 51)

These vivid, macabre incidents are valuable for the insight they gave to the way country people responded (or didn't respond) to the country's great events (the young apprentice regarding the massacre of the Jacobite army as a sideshow, whilst adults carried on 'normal' life in nearby towns; the ostler who only became involved in his country's destiny when someone stole his boots). They reach us through a direct verbal link reaching back almost 120 years before they were finally recorded in written form.

The vignettes, presented to us by Sedgwick, of his neighours, now suffering from the subtle humiliation of an increasing poverty, are powerful not only because of the exactness of the observation, but for the compassion with which he notes the suffering:

> I well remember that, about 75 years since, several poor old men came to the church on Sundays with coats of ancient cut, and adorned on the ample sleeves with curiously embossed metal buttons; with wigs that were once well dressed, with hats of ample brim, shewing the loops that had, in former days drawn the brims up into a smart triple cock; and above all with manners and address which were the tokens of better days... Changes such as those above described can never happen without much physical suffering and some moral mischief... They are among the hard trials of our humanity. But God knows how to draw general good out of partial evil; and by His guiding Providence our mis-

fortunes may become not only his schools of a wise experience but also of true Christian love. (Sedgwick, 1868: x)

There was old Leonard Sedgwick, his father's cousin, who used to travel on horseback to London to deal with the traders of Cheapside, and told young Adam, astride his knee, of the sights of London. There was Thomas Waddington 'a dealer in hats, cloths, drugs and I know not what besides', in whose shop the statesmen met to discuss 'the politics of the day and the affairs of the parish'; Thomas Archer, 'the prince of rural tailors', who would 'work for a few weeks on a London tailor's shop-board' before returning to Dent to provide the statesmen with the latest fashions in decorated coat sleeves; and Blackburne, the barber and wig-maker who specialized in 'three-decker' wigs, and the 'formidable tie-wig with a tail like that of a dragon' called by schoolboys 'the flying dragon':

> All such capital monuments of art were turned out in their glory by the man who with cunning hand and head had built up the crowning decorations of our countrymen. The place of his ancient shop was marked by a great pole, with its symbolical fillet and basin; which I used, in my childhood, to look up to with respectful wonder. But the genius of the place was gone; and I saw only the decayed monuments of the great wig-maker's constructive skill.
>
> I have not stated such facts as these that I might hold up our ancestors of a former century to ridicule; but in the hope of giving my countrymen a graphic proof of the great change of manners wrought by time: and of a sorrowful change in the fortunes of the inhabitants of Dent, that drove many of them away from their early homes, and sank others into a state of depression against which they knew not how to struggle. I well remember (and I first made the remark in my very childhood) that many of the old fashioned dresses, seen on a holiday, were the signs of poverty rather than of pride. The coats were threadbare, and worn by men who had seen better days. The looped broadbrim was seen, but as a sign of mourning, like a flag hoisted half-mast high, for it was the half fallen state of the triple cock (still worn by one or two in the parish) with its three outer surfaces pointing to the sky. And in the same days, old Blackburne's full-bottoms had lost all their crisp symmetry; and the lower hairs of their great convexity were drooping, as if in sorrow, upon the wearers' necks. The three deckers showed broken lines and disordered rigging; and as for the flying dragons, they had all, like autumnal swallows, taken themselves away. But there were many exceptions to these mournful signs of decay. There still remained many Dalesmen with old fashioned dresses, and with cheerful, prosperous looks, among the Sunday congregations at Dent; but the ancient fashions were wearing fast away. (Sedgwick, 1868: 64)

There could, in fact, still be a considerable elegance among the ladies and at least an awareness of the fashions of the times:

> The dress of the upper Statesman's wife and daughters was perhaps less costly than that of the men who affected fashion; and according to modern taste we should call it stiff and ugly to the last degree; as was the fashion of the day. There was one exception however, both as to cost and beauty: for the Statesman's wife often appeared at Church in the winter season in a splendid long cloak of the finest scarlet cloth, having a hood lined with coloured silk. This dress was very becoming, and very costly; but it was carefully preserved, and so it might pass down from mother to daughter. Fortunately, no genius in female decoration (like the Archers and Blackburnes of the other sex) seemed to have brought patches and hoops into vulgar use (as in the preposterous modern case of crinoline).
>
> Among the old Statesmen's daughters hoops did however sometimes appear, as one of the rarer sights of the olden time: and I have heard an aged Statesman's daughter tell of her admiration, and perhaps her envy, when she saw a young woman sailing down the Church with a petticoat that stretched almost across the middle aisle. That decoration shut her out from a seat on any of the Church forms: but by a dexterous flank-movement she won a position among the pews; and then, by a second inexplicable movement, the framework became vertical and found a resting place by overtopping the pew-door—to the great amazement of the rural congregation. (Sedgwick, 1868: 69–70)

There was also a remarkably high degree of literacy among the womenfolk of the Dale, astonishing when formal educational opportunities for girls were so limited. This was extended to a genuine interest in literature; an interest which extended to Defoe and Richardson, even though Sedgwick might deplore the 'sentimental parties' who would weep over the fate of Clarissa Harlowe:

> All the women with very rare exceptions learned to read; and the upper Statesmen's daughter could write and keep family accounts. They had their Bibles, and certain old-fashioned Books of Devotion and they had their Cookery Books; and they were often well read in ballad poetry, and in one or two of De Foe's novels. And some of the younger and more refined of the Statesmen's daughters would form a little clique, where they met—during certain years of last century—and wept over Richardson's novels. But this sentimental portion was small in number; and it produced no effect upon the rural manners of the Valley; which were fresh and cheerful, and little tinged with any dash of what was sentimental.
> (Sedgwick, 1868: 70)

Above anything else, this tightly knit community provided what Sedgwick describes as a 'social compact' within a neigbourhood, a sharing of experience, of mutual help and support in times of joy or grief:

Dent Church.

In all the turns of life the habits of our countrymen were gregarious. A number of houses within certain distances of one another were said to be in the *lâtingrâ* (the seeking row), and formed a kind of social compact. In joy or sorrow they were expected to afford and given help and comfort ... I may mention, how it told upon the customs of Dent, on occasions of great domestic joy. Before the birth of a new inhabitant of the hamlet, all the women of mature life within the *lâtingrâ* had been on the tip-toe of joyful expectation: and the news of the first wailing (the *Crying-out* as called in the tongue of Dent)—the sign of coming life—ran through the home circle like the fiery cross of the Highlanders: and were it night or day, calm sunshine or howling storm, away ran the matrons to the house of promise: and there with cordials and creature comforts, and blessings, and gossip, and happy omens, and with no fear of coming event (for the women of the valley were lively, like the women in the land of Goshen they waited till the infant *Statesman* was brought into this world of joy and sorrow in as much publicity as if he were the heir to the throne of an empire). (Sedgwick, 1868: 73)

And there were indeed, times when such a 'social compact' was desperately necesary; for example, during the Napoleonic Wars when a hitherto unimagined degree of suffering affected the people of the valley:

> I was still living at the parsonage at the end of last century; and I well remember the two years of terrible suffering when the necessaries of life were almost at a famine price, and when many of the farmers and landowners—before that time hardly able to hold up their heads—had to pay poor-rates that were literally more than ten times the weight of what they had been in former years. It was indeed a time of sorrow and great suffering. (Sedgwick, 1868: 77–8)

The support, therefore, provided by neighbours was a necessity.

Not all Dentdale's older customs were as useful as the lâtingrâ. Elsewhere, Sedgwick hints at the 'tales of broad humour' which lead to 'acts of coarse extravagance' which, perhaps sadly, an elderly Victorian clergyman could not, at least in print, repeat. But, typical of the man, though he felt he would be 'ill-employed' were he to dwell on the 'by-gone vices and follies' of his countrymen, he would be 'disloyal to the cause of truth were I only to hold up to the light of day the fairer and brighter side of their character'. Accordingly, he reports the fights sponsored by the Master of the Grammar School in return for an annual 'cock-penny' each Shrovetide which produced 'gambling quarrels, drunken riots and bellowings of blasphemy'. 'Thank God, they have gone out of sight, and will never again, I trust, defile the light of day.' (Sedgwick, 1868: 76).

Typically, Sedgwick, with his puritanical streak, was delighted to note the demise of such 'grotesque and barbarous' usages of a former age, witnessed in his infancy, such as morris dances, rapier dances and mask dances. He recalled, too, the last horse race ever run on the ancient Dent Racecourse, run in his 'very early boyhood', noting that as now the old ground was cut up and changed it would be 'happily' impossible to run the races again should an interest revive.

The economic decline of Dent, however, also brought a social and moral decline. Poverty brought demoralization. If emigration to the new industrial centres of England, to the colonies and to the United States finally relieved the suffering in the valley, those that remained suffered increased hardship. The isolation of the valley increased the effect of depopulation—lawlessness took over. What Sedgwick described as the 'bonds of social and religious union' were 'snapped asunder' and an 'ill-informed and disorderly generation' replaced the old close-knit community.

> I will add a few words more upon the social decline of my countrymen, which no ingenuity on their part could have averted: for the gigantic progress of mechanical and manufacturing skill utterly crushed and swept away the little fabric of industry that had been reared in Dent. Many of the inhabitants gradually sunk into comparative poverty. The silken threads that had held society together began to fail; and lawless manners

followed. There was no longer a Magistrate among the *Statesmen* of Dent, and none of the gentlemen of Sedbergh would qualify for the Bench: and at that time no Magistrate of Westmoreland acted for the outlying portion of Yorkshire. The consequence was, that a parish officer could not communicate with a Magistrate without a rough journey of forty or fifty miles. (Sedgwick, 1868: 77)

It was for this reason that Sedgwick's sisters in 1813, founded a Sunday School in the valley and the Chapel was eventually built at Cowgill. By the 1860s the forces that had brought destruction to the Statesmen's Commonwealth also brought beneficent change. Improved communications and better education restored something of the old confidence to the Dale. There was some new industry— the Dent marble works flourished in the mid-nineteenth century, and the new railways (the Midland Railway's Settle–Carlisle line built in the 1870s was soon to come to Denthead) promised further improvements:

Education has made good progress. Roads are greatly improved. Railroads are touching the extremities of the valley, and are greatly benefiting the farmers of our Dale. We are not now so isolated in England as we once were. The markets are reviving; and again there is hope and cheerfulness among my countrymen. (Sedgwick, 1868: 78)

But the 'mountain republic' was no more.

Adam Sedgwick's relationship with the community of his birth was a subtle and ambivalent one. There can be little doubt that he alway recognized the need to escape from the claustrophobic existence, which a life in the Dale would have meant to him. He won his position of independence at Cambridge after fighting what he confessed were 'hard battles of the brain'. Only when that independence, that freedom, was assured could he return to enjoy 'the true-hearted greetings of my countrymen'.

However, in spite of spending most of his life at Cambridge and later Norwich, the Dale remained a spiritual focal point for him:

For more than threescore years Cambridge has been my honoured resting-place; and here God has given me a life-long task amidst a succession of intellectual friends. For Trinity College, ever since I past under its great portal, for the first time, in the autumn of 1804, I have felt a deep and grateful sentiment of filial regard. But spite of a strong and enduring regard for the University and the College, whenever I have revisited the hills and dales of my native country, and heard the cheerful greetings of my old friends and countrymen, I have felt a new swell of emotion, and said to myself, here is the land of my birth; this was the home of my boyhood, and is still the home of my heart. (Sedgwick, 1868: vi)

The Statesmen of Dent

Long absence, and his eminence as a scholar, academic and clergyman inevitably alienated him from this community. This sense of alienation increased as, in old age, his friends and acquaintances of those boyhood days disappeared. What emerges from the *Memorial* is a loneliness.

Typical of Sedgwick, this is revealed as part of a serious and relatively objective study on Dentdale manners. The direct and 'homely' speech of the Statesmen (a quality noted by others in Sedgwick himself) also involved the use of the Christian name as a signal of recognition to an acquaintance that they too belonged to that community and that, whatever their relative wealth or position, they were equal 'brothers' in that special community. Thus the informal greeting, in an age when formal modes of greeting were the general rule of civilized intercourse, corresponded to what the sociolinguists would describe as a 'Code'. Its contemporary equivalent still survives in certain areas of west and south Yorkshire, and in the Yorkshire Dales and involves the use of the pronoun 'thee' or 'thou'.

> The ancient Statesman and his family had no polish derived from friction with the outer world; but their manners were frank and cheerful, and their address had a native and homely courtesy (springing out of a feeling of independence and hearty good-will) which were very charming. They never passed a neighbour, or even a stranger, without some homely words of kind greeting. Such was the ancient manner of all ranks through the 17th and 18th centuries, as far as I can collect from my own remembrance, and from the traditions of those who loved the Dales and knew the people well. To their Pastor, and to the Master of the grammar-school, or to a stranger, they did not grudge any known address of courtesy: but among themselves the salutations were at once simple, frank, and kind; and they used only the Christian name to a Dalesman, no matter what his condition in life. To have used a more formal address would have been to treat him as a stranger, and unkindly to thrust him out from the Brotherhood of the Dales. And were they not right in this?—What name is so kind and loving as the dear Chistian name, excepting the still dearer and more revered names of Father and Mother? They are the names by which we speak to our brother or sister or friend who is near our hearts. (Sedgwick, 1870: 44)

It came, therefore, as something of a shock to Sedgwick to realize that whilst Adam o' th' Parsons was, of course, a member of this Brotherhood, the Reverend Professor Sedgwick was not. As old friends died, he no longer truly belonged:

> In former times I never returned to Dent without hearing my Christian name uttered with cheerful face and rung with merry voice by all the upgrown persons whom I encountered on the highway. But nearly all my

old friends are gone; and, to my deep sorrow, I no longer hear my Christian name, but am welcomed by words that pronounce me to be a stranger, and no longer a brother living in the hearts of the Dalesmen.
(Sedgwick, 1870: 45)

For this reason, when, in later years, he met an old acquaintance, it mattered a great deal to him that he should be remembered as he was, of them. For instance, Peggy Beckett, childhood playmate, changed her manner and her dialect, significantly, when she recognized the eminent old scholar, who was, after all, really only 'Adam':

There were in my childhood two well known, cheerful-mannered women living in Dent—a mother and daughter employed in the carrying trade—old Peggy Beckett and young Peggy Beckett. Young Peggy won my child's heart by playing with me, and helping me to leap over the tombstones in the churchyard. But she married and disappeared from Dent; and many years, I think not less than seventy, passed away before in exteme old age she returned to Dent, to end her days at her son's cottage. The first time I found my way to Dent after her return, I went, along with some nieces, to call upon her. She received our party with a bright and respectful cheerfulness; but perhaps with more formality than was usual in the Dale; and she spoke to me as a stranger. But when they told her who I was, her fine old face lighted up. She looked earnestly at me for about two seconds, and then said 'Oh Adam, it is lang sin' I tought ye to loup off Battersby's trough!' (Oh Adam it is long since I taught you to leap off Battersby's tombstone.)

This address brought back to my memory a pleasant passage in the life of my childhood; and it proved that the young Peggy Beckett of early years, by this use of my Christian name, no longer thought me a stranger, but welcomed me again as a brother of the Dale. (Sedgwick, 1870: 46)

The example of the old soldier in the Union workhouse again makes this point, with even greater poignancy. It also reveals a further aspect of Sedgwick's deep compassion and humanity. The remarkable part of the little episode lies not so much in the fact that the old veteran should recognize an eminent Professor as a 'brother' in the Dentdale scene, but indeed that Sedgwick, now a world-famous scholar and a busy man of letters, who frequently suffered bouts of ill-health to an extent which would have been enough to allow him to excuse himself from any appointment that he didn't especially need to keep, should not only send an allowance for tobacco or grog, but should find time to go into the dismal surroundings of the local workhouse:

There was an, aged soldier in Dent, poverty-stricken and desolate; having neither wife nor daughter to cheer him. Several times I gave him a trifle by way of remembrance when I visited Dent; and for awhile he had from me a small weekly allowance for tobacco. When in extreme old age he was removed to the Union Workhouse; and he then requested me to exchange the tobacco for a small daily glass of grog.

In the discipline of his regiment he had learned a more smart and formal address than was usual in the Dales; but all this wore away when he tried to express his thanks to me, whenever I called on him. I was then sure to hear my Christian name sounded from his aged lips. The last time I saw him he was above ninety years of age and bedridden, yet apparently happy and in good hope: and when the master of the Union made him understand that a gentleman had called to see him, he said, 'Is it Adam?' I did not remain long with him; and as I left him he pressed my hand and said, 'Oh Adam it is good of you to come and see me here!' (Sedgwick, 1870: 45-6)

Such a concern was typical of Sedgwick and fully in character with the man. Nonetheless, it is clear that a level of involvement with the people of the Dale was important to him. It provided an assurance, an identity which no amount of public recognition elsewhere could quite match.

Adam Sedgwick's own personality, his forthrightness, his Broad Church radicalism, his sometimes rather simplistic way of distinguishing right from wrong—a kind of innocence—his generosity his warmth, his vivid and homely descriptive powers were all qualities which, if they apeared somewhat surprising and even a little alarming to the sophisticated academics of an ancient University, would, among a gathering of Dent statesmen seem satisfyingly typical.

4

John Dawson of Garsdale

Richard Sedgwick would soon realize that his third child, Adam, was 'a lad above common', who would require more intellectual stimulus than the limited curriculum of Dent Grammar School could provide. Not surprisingly he chose to send him, as he had already sent his older son Tom, to his own old school at Sedbergh. Accordingly, in 1799, at the age of 16, Adam was boarded out with two schoolfellows with a local Quaker family, called Foster, friends of the Sedgwick's, who lived at The Hill, just on the edge of Winder Fell, above Sedbergh. They were an honest family and as Sedgwick recalled in later years: 'We were treated with infinite kindness by the family and our happy freedom made us the envy of our school fellows.' (Sedgwick, 1870: 55)

This practice of boarding boys in licensed lodgings was common; accommodation was limited at the Master's House, and although it may have been theoretically possible for Adam to have made the journey each day to and from Dent, Richard Sedgwick clearly would have been grateful for a little additional space at the Parsonage for a family entering their teens.

At this time, the School was housed in the fine neoclassical building on the Dent road which is now the School Library. This building was erected in 1716. The school had enjoyed an excellent academic reputation in the early and mid-eighteenth century. It had a close relationship with St John's College, Cambridge; the sixteenth century founder of the school, Roger Lupton, an influential courtier of both Henry VII and Henry VIII, who had given his birthplace the rich endowment for a school, also ensured a continuing link with St John's by decreeing that the Master of the School 'is to be for ever chosen by the Master of St John's Cambridge' (Clarke and Weech, 1925: 245). There were also a number of scholarships and fellow-

John Dawson of Garsdale

Sedbergh School as it was in 1800. The building is now the School Library.

ships appropriated to the school.

To a large extent, however, the reputation of the school depended on the success or otherwise of the Master. A gifted and inspired teacher could develop the school into a centre of excellence, and a large number of local boys gained entrance to the academic professions under the direction of such men as Posthumous Wharton (held office 1674–1706) and Dr Samuel Saunders (held office 1746–1782). It is noteworthy in fact that local boys of limited means were able to attend the school as payments were not exacted for tutorship except for the fact that:

> it had been a generall practice that the parents or other friends of boyes brought to be taught in the said School did give the Master ten shillings or twenty shillings or more or less as their ability or inclinations moved them, for a gratuity when they did first bring boyes [sic] to be taught there. (Clarke and Weech, 1925: 242)

Adam Sedgwick

In practice however, unless a boy had a means of subsistence, even such generosity was irrelevant and a cottager's son, however gifted (and John Dawson will perhaps be the supreme example), would find no simple meritocratic route up to Cambridge. Unlike in Scotland, eighteenth-century education in England was not organized on egalitarian principles. Nonetheless, there was more flexibility in the system than is sometimes supposed, and local boys of limited means, who were talented, could benefit from the generous provisions of Roger Lupton's will at Sedbergh.

If the Mastership was in the hands of a weak or incompetent man, then all, rich and poor alike, suffered. Even the School Governors were powerless, except to 'lament their self-imposed impotence and watch for happier days'.

If the 'inglorious Mastership' of Christopher Hull ended when he collapsed and died in the middle of Sedbergh in 1799, his successor, the Reverend William Stevens, a former Royal Navy Chaplain and veteran of the battle of St Vincent, was only a little better. He was reputed to be a competent scholar and teacher, at least in mathematics, but the school hardly prospered in his time, and in his later years: 'His character grew from sternness to severity and cruelty, and he practised flogging mercilessly. The School House was closed and the few boys in the school were taught in the Masters House' (Clarke and Weech, 1925: 56).

Nonetheless, Richard Sedgwick had sufficient confidence in Stevens to entrust his sons to his care, and they seemed to have made reasonable progress. At the time of his appointment Stevens was a young man of thirty and, although there were only a handful of pupils (a mere 92 pupils entered the School during his 20 year period of office), he must have had hopes of doing something a little better. Adam Sedgwick recalled him as an 'excellent scholar and a good social and domestic man' (Sedgwick, 1870: 65), but also recalled 'there is something about him I neither liked nor understood' (Clark and Hughes, 1890, vol. I: 57).

It is significant that when circumstances finally overwhelmed Stevens, and illness, poverty and suffering, including the death of his wife leaving a large family motherless, led to his own early death in 1819 at the age of 50, it was two old pupils, Miles Bland and the newly appointed Professor Adam Sedgwick, who raised a 'large sum' of money to provide for Stevens' orphaned and destitute children. Only eight pupils remained at the School at the time of Stevens' death.

Nonetheless, Stevens must be given some credit for those distinguished pupils who went through Sedbergh at this period. Included among these were: Miles Bland (1784–1867), referred to above, Second Wrangler at Cambridge, theologian and mathematician in later life; William Ainger (1783–1840), lifelong friend of Adam Sedgwick, Principal of St Bee's Theological College and a Canon of Chester; Robert Baynes Armstrong (1784–1869), again lifelong friend of Sedgwick, Barrister, Recorder of Manchester and Bolton, and MP for Lancaster in 1848; Sedgwick himself; and George Peacock (1791–1858), later colleague of Sedgwick at Trinity and one of the greatest mathematicians and astronomers of his day. Perhaps they were the kind of men who would have succeeded no matter what the circumstances.

The fact that no fewer than six of the relatively few pupils taught by Stevens became classified in that highly competitive and select list of Cambridge scholars known as 'Wranglers' (graduates who had achieved First-Class honours and were listed in order of merit) was not so much due to Reverend Stevens' ability, but to the presence in Sedbergh of a remarkable, self-effacing mathematical genius, John Dawson.

John Dawson was a seminal influence on Adam Sedgwick. He was the family surgeon, his father's own favoured tutor and life-long friend, and it is inevitable that Adam would have seen a good deal of Dawson during his time in Sedbergh before formally becoming his pupil in 1804 after being accepted as a Sizar at Cambridge.

Dawson's career was so astonishing, that it deserves some fuller explanation. He was born in late January or early February 1734, the younger of two sons, to William and Mary Dawson of Raygill Farm, Garsdale. Poor as his 'statesman' father was, the sons were able to get a little basic literacy at the Reverend Charles Udale's school, Garsdale. His older brother was given further help so that he could perhaps get a post 'with the excise', whilst it was considered more appropriate for John to learn husbandry.

However, John soon left Garsdale school owing to the 'severity' of treatment he had received, and continued his education by borrowing his brother's books. As a youngster he had to contribute to the work of the farm, cutting turf and peat for fuel from the hillside above the farm and tending his father's sheep. He was allowed, however, to use his 'knitting brass'—the money he earned from manufacture of knitted garments whilst tending flocks—for the purchase of books bought on the occasional trip into Sedbergh.

A contemporary has provided a vivid picture of his method of study and the hardship it caused him:

> His principal time for study was in winter, after the trials of the day

Adam Sedgwick

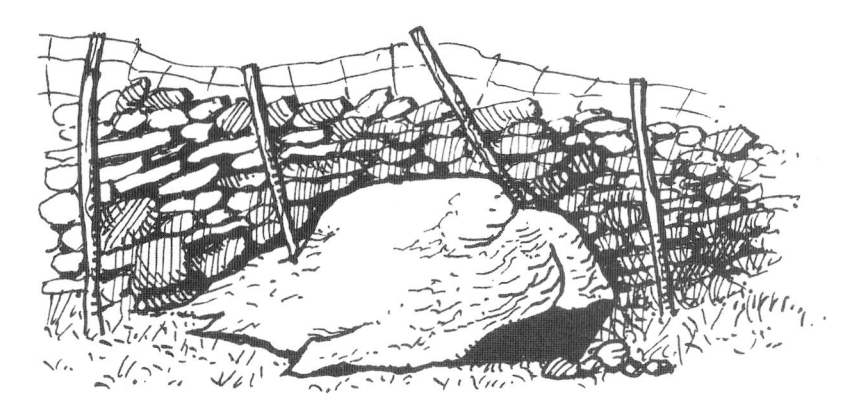

Dawson's Rock, Garsdale.

were closed, at these hours he had no other light but that of a peat fire, situated on the floor—what are called by the country people, heath fires—the painful stooping posture necessary for availing himself of this light, occasioned a violent bleeding of the nose, which, for more than a year prevented him from lying down in bed, and brought him to so low a state of health that his life was despaired of.   (*Lonsdale Magazine*, vol II, no. 13, 1821).

Yet he recovered sufficiently to be able to work out for himself an elaborate system of Conic Sections—a complex and highly original mathematical formula. By tradition this was achieved whilst watching the flocks from a large boulder or out-crop of rock on the fellside high above Garsdale, which is still known as Dawson's Rock.

By his late teens and early twenties he was already getting employment as an itinerant teacher and it is at this time that three students about to enter Cambridge came to seek his help. One of these was John Haygarth, also of Garsdale, later to become a famous surgeon in Leeds; another was Richard Sedgwick who had cause to remember his 'Garsdale summer'. This was in 1756.

When he was 23 or 24, he became an apprentice to one Dr Bracken, a surgeon and apothecary of Lancaster, continuing to study mathematics, optics and philosophy whilst learning medicine. He quickly picked up the essentials of the surgeon's craft to such good effect that at the end of this period he was able to set up in Sedbergh as a badly needed local surgeon and apothecary. He lived frugally and by the end of the year he had saved up £100. Needing further, formal qualifications, he stitched this money into the lining of his waistcoat and set off, staff in hand, to walk across the fells to Edinburgh. The Scottish system of 'open' Universities on the Continental pattern allowed a poor student to afford lectures, which he did by living in a cheap garret and in 'sternest self-denial' until his money ran out, after which he walked back to Sedbergh to continue practising medicine among the local community until he could finance further formal study.

Again, his practical skills were such that the practice flourished and soon he saved up around £300. This time he went to London, travelling partly on foot and partly by humble carrier's wagon, the usual means of conveyance for the poor, again with his wealth stitched up in 'small parcels under his waistcoat'.

Whilst he was able to attend 'one good course of surgical lectures' and obtain a diploma, he soon found life much more expensive than in Sedbergh or Edinburgh. But his outstanding mathematical gifts were being widely recognized and he was already being sought out by leading men of science and letters.

Typically, Dawson chose to return to a 'useful' life in Yorkshire. He returned to Sedbergh, married a local girl, Ann Thirnbeck, of Ellers, and set up an excellent local medical practice 'attending the sick, helping the dying, delivering women in childbirth, occupying himself with the manifold duties of a country doctor' (Booth, 1970). His excellence as a doctor is not only evidenced by the wide and lasting reputation he enjoyed among the local community, but by his willingness to put the newest scientific principles in practice. Dr John Haygarth, his old pupil, was one of the great pioneers of 'isolation, cleanliness and ventilation' in the treatment of infectious disease. The medical historian, Dr C. C. Booth, notes that a case study from Dawson in 1780 and reported in one of Haygarth's books on smallpox, indicates how the measures adopted by Dawson helped prevent the outbreak of a major smallpox epidemic in Sedbergh:

> Dawson describes the death from confluent smallpox of a young man called John Airey in a fetid, upstairs room in a back street in Sedbergh. His report describes the preventative measures that he took and shows how, despite the fact that many were susceptible, no one else in the town contracted the disease. This was interesting, for it shows that Dawson at that time was following the rules laid down by Haygarth, his fellow Dalesman for the treatment and prevention of infectious fevers. (Booth, 1970)

Clearly, the price of Dawson's involvement in medicine was that eighteenth-century mathematics lost one of its towering intellects, a potential Newton, whose work in mathematics was now confined to a few leisure moments in a crowded life. Not that Dawson would have seen it this way. It is recorded that he 'never struggled for

Adam Sedgwick

reputation—he rather sought to spend his life in obscurity' (*Lonsdale Magazine,* vol II, no. 13, 1821). It is an interesting philosophical point as to whether a life devoted to the physical welfare of a local community as Dawson's was, is of more value than that of a mathematician whose discoveries could have helped change the direction of mathematical and scientific thinking. To Dawson the choice was a theoretical one; without patronage he could not live by mathematics; by medicine he could earn an honest living.

However, there was time for a little study. He engaged in learned correspondence and was able to refute one William Emerson and support one Thomas Simpson in Simpson's view that Newton had made an error in the problem of *precession*. Dawson achieved the proof by means of an adroit mathematical analysis. Or more spectacularly, in an anonymous pamphlet published in 1769, the country doctor demolished the elaborate mathematical theory of Matthew Stewart, Professor of Mathematics at the University of Edinburgh, which suggested that the distance of the Sun from the Earth could be calculated by using the theory of gravity, and observing the effects of gravitational pull on the orbit of the moon. Dawson demonstrated mathematically that this could not be done and, in fact, that it was only by careful observation of the orbit of Venus that the Sun's distance could be effectively calculated. James Cook's voyage which began in 1768 to Tahiti provided an opportunity to examine this thesis, and Cook's observations proved Dawson absolutely correct. The fame of this major discovery brought many famous scientists and noblemen to visit Dawson in Sedbergh, including such men as the geologist John Playfair of Edinburgh and Henry (later Lord) Brougham.

It was a question of fitting in pupils literally between duties as a physician; attending to the sick morning and evening and seeing pupils in the afternoons. He retired from full-time medical practice in 1788, but was always ready to help the sick and needy, particularly to use his skills for difficult or urgent cases.

Pupils came from throughout the British Isles to study with Dawson at Sedbergh, paying a tuition fee of some five shillings a week, and arranging their own accommodation. One such pupil, a Dr Butler, later headmaster of Harrow, was taught by Dawson in 1792 and recorded that in addition to the five shillings fee to Dawson, he could stay at the King's Arms in Sedbergh for one and sixpence a week for an excellent room, spending two pence per day for breakfast and ten pence for a dinner consisting of 'a leg of mutton and potatoes, both hot, ham and tongue, gooseberry tarts, cheese, butter and bread' (Booth, 1970). Not only did students preparing to enter University study with Dawson, but undergraduates receiving little help from their own tutors, were forced to receive outside 'coaching' for their final examinations, including the notorious Cambridge Mathematics Tripos. It says sufficient for Dawson's excellence and fame that no fewer than eleven Cambridge 'Senior Wranglers', that is the best mathematician of their year, were Dawson men.

He was an extraordinarily fine teacher. It was noted that 'Such was the mildness of his temper that he was almost idolised by his scholars who at one point combined to subscribe an "elegant service of plate" in gratitude' (*Lonsdale Magazine*, vol. II, no. 13, 1821). He was a keen country rambler, at a period when walking was too often a necessity to be considered a pleasure; Dawson, it is recorded, was 'particularly partial' to walking for pleasure and exercise, an enthusiasm shared by Adam Sedgwick. His powers of concentration were phenomenal. It was widely rumoured that he could solve the most difficult intellectual problems riding to patients on horseback. And he had the power of complete mental absorption:

> his friends have often seen him read, with vivacity indeed, but without any apparent effort of mind, books of profoundest mathematics, by his own fire sat amidst the noise of conversation; when his countenance would brighten, and his hand would strike the arm of his chair, in token of the pleasure he received from the elegance of the author's demonstration, or the depth of his researches. (*Lonsdale Magazine*, vol II, no. 13, 1821)

Adam Sedgwick shared in the 'idolisation' of this gentle but uncompromising man. Something of Dawson's extraordinary intellectual integrity and enthusiasm lit a flame in the mind of the young scholar, that remained undimmed throughout a long and active life. He always remembered that first 'Garsdale summer' as perhaps the moment of his first real intellectual awakening. A great teacher is a creative force that goes beyond the particular discipline. Moral values and standards are involved, which can go to the very root of a person's being. To some extent Adam Sedgwick spent a great deal of the rest of his life trying to live up to those standards of John Dawson's. It is not without significance that a portrait of his old teacher remained in Sedgwick's rooms in Cambridge throughout his career, and that he left, at the end of his own life, a vivid and moving tribute to Dawson which gives an impression, and this cannot be accidental, remarkably similar to that recorded by people meeting Sedgwick himself:

> Simple in manners, cheerful and mirthful in temper with a dress

John Dawson of Garsdale.

approaching that of the higher class of venerable old Quakers of the Dales without any stuffiness or affectation of superiority, yet did he bear at first sight a very commanding presence, and it was impossible to glance at him for a moment without feeling that we were before one whom God has given gifts above those of a common man. His powerful projecting forehead and well chiselled features told of much thought; and might have implied severity, had not a soft radiant benevolence played over his fine old face, which inspired his friends, of whatever age or rank, with confidence and love.   (Sedgwick, 1870: 54)

Even more moving is the last meeting Sedgwick had with his old teacher, a short time before the latter's death at the advanced age of 86. In spite of the fact that the aged man was now a 'veritable intellectual ruin', something of the old power and clarity remained; the portrait is both tragic and yet, like Wordsworth's leech-gatherer of

Resolution and Independence giving an impression of great human dignity and courage; the old scholar calmly accepting the realities of his situation:

> The last time I saw him was in extreme old age, not long before his death. His memory was shaken, and I was told by his daughter (who was the prop and solace of his latter years) that he would not be able to sustain any long, connected conversation. But to my surprise and joy, he lighted up, talked of old times and early studies, and then, with all his former earnestness of expression, and clearness of thought, he spoke of the introduction of the powerful French mathematical analysis into the Cambridge course; and he named with great precision some analytical works which he had read within the last two or three years. 'I have sometimes grieved' he said, 'but perhaps it is ungrateful of me, that I did not know this powerful implement of discovery early in life. I thought I might have grasped it, and then tried my hand with some of the great problems of physical astronomy; but I am now a feeble old man, and my days are nearly numbered.' It was in truth one of the last flickerings of his intellectual life and love. I saw him again, the same day, and endeavoured to bring his mind back to the previous conversation. But in vain. His mental power had gone; and he seemed to have no remembrance of the subjects, which a very little while before had drawn from him such bright gleams of intellectual life. (Sedgwick, 1870: 51)

John Dawson died on September 19th, 1820 and is buried in Sedbergh. A fine marble bust was placed in Sedbergh Church by his friends. The inscription reads:

> In memory of John Dawson of Sedbergh...
> Distinguished by his profound knowledge of mathematics,
> beloved for his aimiable simplicity of character, and
> revered for his exemplary discharge of every moral and
> religious duty.

5

Cambridge: a crisis of identity

It might have been expected, because of the long and close association of Sedbergh School with St John's, that Adam Sedgwick, when he went to Cambridge, would have been sent there. However, it had been agreed between Mr Stevens, his father and the Reverend Peacock, Vicar of Sedbergh, that Trinity would be a better choice, supposedly because his schoolfellow Miles Bland, who was already down for St John's, was the cleverer of the two and this would reduce Sedgwick's chances of ultimately obtaining a Fellowship. Accordingly, he was entered as a sizar of Trinity College under the tutorship of Mr Thomas Jones, on November 18th, 1803, and had ten months to prepare himself for university at school and under the guidance of Mr Dawson.

The system of sizarship requires a little explanation. Basically it was a kind of scholarship; sizars were usually selected from a group of subsizars, by examinations. Sizarships were definitely reserved for scholars of limited means, particularly sons of clergymen, and the value of a sizarship at the beginning of the nineteenth century was around £150 per annum, a considerable sum in those days, but probably only adequate to see an undergraduate through a year at college (Rothblatt, 1968).

On September 29th, 1804, therefore, Miles Bland and Adam Sedgwick left Dent for Kirkby Stephen, staying overnight with a friend before catching the 'Paul Jones' coach at Brough, and travelling for three days and two 'dismal' nights before reaching Cambridge.

It is difficult to imagine the immediate impact his new surroundings must have had on Sedgwick, who had previously never travelled beyond Carlisle. The majestic architecture of the ancient colleges, the beauty of the riverside 'backs' and the sophistication of the academic community must have made a considerable impression. It is recorded that he was regarded as a slightly uncouth adolescent, provincial in dress and manners, sober in habits, and doubtless with a fairly broad Dentdale accent. But as an earnest ambitious scholar he would quickly become disenchanted with many of his fellow-students, sons of the aristocracy for whom Cambridge was little more than a pleasant diversion. As one modern commentator has expressed it:

> As for the undergraduates, who were dismally few in number, their real interest in shooting, riding, boating, violence and gambling was hardly at all distracted by the ultimate necessity to scramble parrot Latin through some meaningless exercises of medieval descent in order to qualify for a pass degree. (Hall, 1969: 2)

In many respects, Cambridge in 1804 was at a nadir. It was conservative, even by its own standards, complacent and singularly remote from any genuine habits of research or intellectual invention. The Dissenting Academics (dissenters were excluded from the University because of religious 'Tests'), Joseph Priestley in Birmingham, John Dalton in Manchester, men like Playfair or Jameson in Edinburgh were at the frontiers of knowledge. In Cambridge a rigid curriculum centred almost exclusively on mathematics and the classics, hedged around following traditional attitudes and procedures that owed more to Aristotle than Francis Bacon, and stifled originality and any creative talent.

There was another reason too, for a shortage of scholars. The Napoleonic Wars were at their height, and the possibility of a French invasion was very real. The economic effects of the war were such that few could afford the luxury of a university education. In 1804 only 128 young men entered for matriculation, compared with an average of over 150 for the period and over 200 for the succeeding decade after peace had been declared.

However, Sedgwick was fortunate to have a capable tutor the Reverend Thomas Jones. Jones was an able scholar, and good teacher. His work with Sedgwick was effective enough to enable Sedgwick to distinguish himself by being one of only six students to be entered in the first class when the College examinations were held in June 1805. These examinations included a formidable vica voce held in the Hall of Trinity in front of the Master, and must have been an extraordinarily demanding experience for a shy first-year student.

It must, therefore, have been with considerable satisfaction that Sedgwick returned to Dent in the summer of 1805, taking the news of his initial success back to John Dawson, particularly as the success was as convincing in classics as in mathematics. In accordance with University regulations about private tutorships, Dawson was permitted to coach Sedgwick during the summer vacation. It was, as always, a highly profitable period of study.

Shortly after his return to Cambridge in the Autumn however, he contracted typhoid fever. The illness developed with dramatic speed and at one time his life was despaired of. Fortunately, the crisis passed; his constitution proved strong enough to withstand the strain and he recovered. He was, however, confined to his room for over four months, yet typically insisted on being carried to his window in November 1805 to see the celebrations in Cambridge to mark Nelson's victory at Trafalgar (Clark and Hughes, 1890, vol. I: 78).

In spite of the debilitating effect of his illness, he was still able to be classified in the first class list in the College examinations that summer.

There is tantalizingly little record of Sedgwick's life at this period, most of the many letters he wrote home to Dent having been lost or destroyed. What does emerge, however, is a figure who, in a curious way, has a contemporary equivalent; the scholarship boy, hardworking, highly ambitious, single minded, establishing himself by the one certain method he knew how—academic excellence.

Degree examinations at that time in Cambridge followed an archaic and legalistic system of 'disputation' in which students had to argue erudite and scholastic dissertations, in Latin, with an examiner or Moderator assessing the brilliance of a student's performance in demolishing the arguments of his opponents. There were also written papers in various subjects. The series of examinations began in the third year, finally ending with a Senate House examination. The written part of the Tripos, as it was known, consisted of examinations in arithmetic, geometry, trigonometry, mechanics, optics, astronomy, and of course, Newton's *Principia*; it stressed method—excellence of technique, precision in thought, logic, intellectual vigour. The principle behind it was that he who could master its complex skills had the intellectual capacity to master any subject and it was, clearly, a demanding intellectual test. It was a useful device, too, for controlling students who, at least in their final year, were forced to cram an extraordinary amount of somewhat useless knowledge in order to compete for Honours. As Rothblatt (1968: 182) points out: 'Nowhere was there a suggestion of original synthesis, analysis or a developing fountain of knowledge'.

There seems little doubt that Sedgwick had serious hopes of being Senior Wrangler, and there is evidence to suggest that certain of the

College Fellows expected him to head the list. But after the final trial, Sedgwick's name stood Fifth; as prophesied by his old schoolmaster he was in fact beaten by Miles Bland, who was Second Wrangler.

It is significant that whilst he was preparing for his degree Sedgwick's elder sister Margaret had written to him, noting their father's increasing problems with his sight, which were now so severe that 'he fears he shall not be able to teach the school next winter', and including the ominous words 'How will you like to be Dent's schoolmaster?' As Sedgwick wrote to his friend William Ainger:

> if my Father's sight should continue to decline, a fixed residence in Dent must be my inevitable lot. This situation above all others I should dislike. Little as I have seen of the world, I have seen enough to find that to me no pleasures are to be found in illiterate solitude. (Clark and Hughes, 1890, vol. I: 92)

At this stage, he still had hoped of reading for the Bar, but he lacked the means. The necessity now was to obtain a Fellowship of his College, obtained by means of a further taxing and highly competitive examination.

During the vacation, there was an opportunity to earn a little additional money by teaching a summer 'reading-party' of undergraduates, but after another year's study he failed to win the desperately needed Fellowship. This was in the autumn of 1809. Only two vacant Fellowships were available, and a rival candidate, a less able mathematician than Sedgwick, but producing a brilliant translation from Pindar into English verse, excelled Sedgwick in classics to claim one of the coveted places. It meant, therefore, waiting another whole year before, in October 1810, Sedgwick, having painstakingly improved his knowledge of Latin verse obtained one of the four Fellowships offered that year by the College.

Judging by the letters of congratulations from his colleagues, it was clearly a popular selection, for 'Sedge', as he was known, was already a personality at Trinity. But no letter could have given him more pleasure than the post-script to a letter from his old schoolmaster which simply noted that 'Mr Dawson begs to join the congratulations'.

What did a Fellowship mean? It was, to a degree, independence and security, 'an agreeable membership of a club until such time as the Fellow passed on to a Church living or marriage'.

It was a pleasant, privileged way of life in a civilized environment, and now, not only had the spectre of returning to Dent as schoolmaster diminished, but he was no longer a burden on his parents and the education of his two brothers would be facilitated. As a Fellow, he could expect to earn a useful living from the extensive system of private tutorship in Cambridge at the time. Formal College lectures were of little direct value to students working for competitive examinations. Accordingly during vacations and even in term time private arrangements were made whereby a lecturer, a Fellow, or a graduate kept from a Fellowship because of marriage (Fellowships were strictly for bachelors) could train students in the elaborate system of intellectual gymnastics required to perform successfully in the Mathematics Tripos. The system was self-perpetuating because it benefited Fellows too, as Rothblatt has suggested, the 'cramming' system for all its faults was 'the only practical school of education in Cambridge, the only place where a prospective university teacher could prove his worth in a competitive situation'. (Rothblatt, 1968)

Even more to the point, the income was one of the few ways in which a poor scholar, like Adam Sedgwick, could pay his way.

However, there was a price. The years of intensive study, for the College examinations, for his degree and finally for his Fellowship, told on his physical and mental well-being. He had lost weight—it was noted by one of his friends that he had lost two or three stones. Moreover, the Fellowship did not prove to be as agreeable as he had hoped. His teaching duties were unrewarding, working, as he had to, with pupils with little or no genuine interest in mathematics 'Six of the blessed youths,' he records 'I have to feed each day' and his own enthusiasm for mathematics declined with the daily drudgery of teaching; reading in other subjects was reduced dramatically. He began to deplore his wasted life, and even considered leaving Cambridge in order to have done with the system altogether.

Many of his contemporaries at Cambridge had by now left. He missed his old friends; there were few congenial companions among the Fellows, who were, for the most part, a dull and narrow-minded group. He was aware that it was necessary for him to be ordained, if he wished to remain in academic life or obtain a living in the Church, but had little enthusiasm for theology. Above all he had a sense of time being wasted. He lived under an almost continuous state of depression, a gloom relieved only by summer 'reading parties' with students, such as one at Bury St Edmunds in 1811, and another at Lowestoft.

His characteristic mood of despondency is clearly revealed in a letter to William Ainger February 14th, 1812:

> Here I am grinding away with six pupils. Under such circumstances it is impossible to advance one step. But I am compelled by circumstances to

undergo this drudgery. When I look back on what I have done since I was elected Fellow I cannot discover that I have made any proficiency whatever, or gained one new idea. (Clark and Hughes, 1890, vol I: 102)

The collapse came as the result of a river trip in May 1813. A neglected cold led to an attack of acute bronchitis, and his health broke completely. He was forced to give up his work as a college examiner and after three weeks, having partially recovered, travelled to Dent to convalesce. On the journey home a relapse occurred, and when he finally arrived in Yorkshire his friends were shocked at his appearance. Only two months complete rest, followed by a walking holiday in the Lakes, finally restored his condition, but the effects of his breakdown were to remain with him for the rest of his life.

In later years, he described his experience, and its traumatic effects on him:

> I became alarmingly ill with overwork; I had now been reading hard for 8 or 9 years, and it had told severely upon me. There was honour to be won, and I won it; nor can I altogether regret the sacrifice it cost me, I was 5 years deprived of natural rest in bed, and could only sleep reclining in a chair. (Sedgwick, undated MS.)

He never fully recovered. Sustained intellectual effort from that time on—he was just 27—remained a burden to him. Outdoor activity became absolutely necessary to restore his vitality. It was a mental condition that had physical symptoms, and in Sedgwick's case it was frequently difficult to distinguish between actual bodily ailments and bouts of hypochondria, brought on by long periods of depression. And yet physically he was immensely strong, and could out-walk and out-ride most of his contemporaries, and prove almost immune to fatigue. As his biographers noted, Cambridge itself now brought upon him almost a change of personality, compared with the energetic enthusiast undertaking a walking tour in the Lakes or on the Continent, or rough shooting on the fells above Dent: 'listless as he was at Cambridge, the moment he got to Dent he became a different man' (Clark and Hughes, 1890, vol I: 132).

The condition is one familiar to students of neurotic behaviour, a 'flight into illness' to escape an unpleasant experience. But it was perhaps even more than this. It was an example of what the social psychologist Erik Erikson would term a 'crisis of identity' (Erikson, 1950).

For six years, between 1804 and 1810 he had devoted himself, with single-minded purpose, towards obtaining a specific goal, the prize of a Fellowship. These years of almost monastic study formed what

Erikson terms a 'moratorium' in so far as decisions about his future career and life were postponed. As Fifth Wrangler and a Fellow of Trinity he had identified himself as a scholar; but the drudgery of cramming for examinations and the lack of any genuine intellectual purpose of his own now contrasted sharply with the drive and direction given to him, at the beginning of his academic career, by the 'grand intellect' of John Dawson.

There was progress of a sort. In 1815 he was appointed Assistant Tutor, a post that carried new lecturing responsibilities, an income and made him less dependent on cramming private pupils. Although mathematics no longer were of burning interest to him, he took his duties seriously, and the increased financial independence allowed him to take an extended tour of France, Switzerland, Germany and Holland during the following summer.

By this time Sedgwick had the responsibility of overseeing the progress through Cambridge of his two younger brothers, James and John, and in July 1817, on pain of forfeiting his College Fellowship (a statute of Trinity decreed that all Fellows, except two, should be in Priest's orders within seven years of completing their degree of Master of Arts), Sedgwick completed his theological studies and was ordained a Deacon. It is often naively assumed that Sedgwick's later position on geological questions was dominated by his theological convictions—the 'Reverend' of his title. But there is no evidence that he undertook ordination for any other reason than sheer economic necessity, and whilst his responsibilities as a churchman in later years clearly coloured his viewpoint, at least in his youth his involvement in the Church was mainly that of a poor scholar accepting the only avenue open to him. It was either ordination or expulsion.

However, soon after his ordination in fact, he was helping out with parochial duties in Dent, as well as doing some rough shooting on the local moors, a pastime he continued to enjoy until he became a geologist and 'gave away my dogs and gun, and my hammer broke my trigger.' Again his health was excellent in Dent, but deteriorated as soon as he returned to the routine drudgery of Cambridge. But his duties kept him busy:

> I am as usual employed two hours every morning in lecturing to the men of the first and second year, and every other day we are engaged about two hours and a half more in examining the men of the third year. We are besides employed at least three hours in the evening in looking over their papers.   (Clark and Hughes, 1890, vol. I: 152)

It was a depressing experience and continued to tell on his health. He was urged to resign his lectureship by his relatives. He was now

Trinity College, Cambridge, from a painting by R. B. Harradan, dated 1845. Sedgwick's rooms were in the top floor of the range on the left of the clock tower.

nearly 33, and the crisis of 1813 was still not resolved.

In the Spring of 1818, the Reverend John Hailstone (1759–1847), the Woodwardian Professor of Geology, resigned his Chair. One of the conditions of the founder's will was that the holder of the post should not be distracted by matrimony. At the age of 58, the Reverend Hailstone had decided, no doubt sensibly, to marry. This post was an interesting one. It was established as a result of a generous bequest by John Woodward. Woodward (1665–1728) was a brilliant, if eccentric, scholar, who dabbled in many fields, including medicine, archaeology, botany and field geology, and in particular was perhaps the first scholar fully to appreciate the 'vital importance of field-work in geological studies'.

> The first geologist to work his way, systematically, through the English countryside, seeking out exposures, collecting specimens, and building up from his notebooks a picture of the geology of England which must have been unique in its day.   (Davies, 1969: 83)

In many respects Woodward's observations anticipated the stratigraphical approach pioneered by William Smith in the early years of the following century:

> I made strict enquiry wherever I came, and laid out for intelligence of all

places where the entrails of the earth were laid open, either by nature (if I may so say) or by art and human industry. And wheresoever I go I had notice of any considerable natural spelance or grotto any sinking of wells, or digging for earths, etc. or the like, I forthwith had recourse thereunto. The result was, that in time I was abundantly assured that the circumstances of these things in remote countries were much the same as those of over here.   (Woodward, 1695: 6)

Dr Woodward—parodied as 'Dr Fossile' in John Gay's *Three Hours after Marriage*—made an extensive collection of minerals and fossils, which was unique in its day. When he died, his will instructed that most of his estate should be sold and part of the proceeds used to buy enough land to generate an income of £150 per year. This land was to be entrusted to the University of Cambridge, which would use part of the income to pay the salary of a lecturer, whose duties would include guardianship of the collection of geological specimens bequeathed by Woodward to the University, and at least four lectures annually. The professorship thus established was 'Britain's oldest academic post' (Davies, 1969: 83) in earth sciences, and one of the first posts of its kind in the world.

The requirements of Woodward's Will were not taken equally seriously by all the occupiers of the Woodward Chair, although some, like John Michell (1724–1793), were fine geologists. Charles Mason, for example, occupied the post for 28 years, and, although an active geologist, printed only one Latin lecture; another, the eccentric divine Samuel Ogden, distinguished himself by producing panegyrics to royalty in Latin, English and Arabic (Clark and Hughes, vol. I: 189–93). Compared with these, John Hailstone, who took the post in 1788, was a breath of energy. In 1792 he published the syllabus for a course of lectures and he was also an excellent curator of the Museum, spending a great deal of time and money developing a fine collection of minerals and fossils and building up a library. He did give some lectures, opening the Museum twice a week and attending 'to demonstrate and explain the subjects of this Branch of Natural History to such curious persons or strangers, as are engaged in the study of them' (Cambridge University Calender, 1803).

Unlike a twentieth-century Professor, who is expected to direct a department of scholars engaged in teaching and research, a Cambridge Professor, at the turn of the nineteenth century, worked entirely on his own and his teaching duties, if any, were not related in any way to the examination syllabus of the Univeristy. Any students who came along, came out of curiosity or general intellectual interest. The status of the post was relatively low, and in no way had

Cambridge: a crisis of identity

the glamour and authority which came to be attached to it by late Victorian times.

Nonetheless, the idea of a post away from the tedium of teaching a sterile mathematics syllabus to indifferent undergraduates, a post which offered exciting new possibilities, appealed to Sedgwick's imagination. He decided to seek election. Financially, in fact, the post offered little. The salary was £100 per annum, a pittance even by the standards of that time, and was indeed less than he was currently earning as an Assistant Tutor, but this was irrelevant besides the fact that it offered a challenge to that considerable, and largely frustrated, intellectual energy which he knew he possessed. As he wrote to William Ainger:

> What do you make of the business? If I succeed I shall have a motive for *active* exertion in a way which will promote my intellectual improvement, and I hope make me a happy and useful member of society. I am not such a fool as to suppose my present employment is useless; and my pecuniary prospects are certainly better than they would be were I Woodwardian Professor. Still, as far as the improvement of the mind is considered, I am at this moment doing nothing. Nay, I often seriously think that I am doing worse than nothing; that I am gradually losing that little information I once had, and very sensibly approaching that state of fatuity to which we must all come if we remain here long enough.
> (Clark and Hughes, vol. I: 153–4)

There were three candidates for the post, Robert Wilson Evans, George Cornelius Gorham and Sedgwick. Evans, realizing that support within Trinity was going to be stronger for Sedgwick than for himself, withdrew. Gorham had made some serious study of geology and felt a great sense of injustice at the method of selection, which was by ballot of all the Fellows of the Colleges of the University. As a member of a small College, Queens', he was at some disadvantage against Sedgwick, who could count on almost total support not only from his own College, but from St John's with which he had connections of friendship. Sedgwick, moreover, was a popular personality. His friends organized an effective campaign and in the event, Sedgwick polled 186 votes, whilst Gorham polled 59.

The new Woodwardian Professor is reported to have said with quite disarming frankness: 'I had but one rival, Gorham of Queens' and he had not the slightest chance against me, for I knew absolutely nothing of geology, whereas he knew a good deal—but it was all wrong' (Clark and Hughes, 1890, vol. I: 160).

Again, the remark that is frequently quoted (without source), i.e.

'Hitherto I have never turned a stone; henceforth I will leave no stone unturned', has allowed Sedgwick's detractors, such as Himmelfarb (1959: 33), to confuse an engaging modesty with reality. In fact, there is reason to suppose that Sedgwick had read a certain amount of 'natural philosophy' and would have been well acquainted with the subject in a general way; it would be astonishing if he had not, and for a reasonably intelligent layman, the acquisition of a working acquaintance with current issues in the science would have been a simple matter. The most convincing evidence lies in the fact that Sedgwick was formally 'introduced' to the Geological Society of London on April 19th, 1816, a full two years before his election (Woodward, 1907: 39). Clearly a man with no knowledge at all would be unlikely to attend a learned gathering of this nature, and indeed, having attended, even as a visitor, he would have considerable insight into some of the major geological discussions of the time.

Nonetheless, it must be admitted that Sedgwick's formal geological training was minimal and that his appointment was made more because of his potential as a geologist than any existing achievement. Too often in the past the Woodwardian Professorship had been a mere sinecure. The notion of a bright young man mastering a subject sufficiently well to teach it effectively was not unheard of at the time, and, as has been suggested, a Professorial Chair lacked that sense of authority and scholarship which later would have made such an appointment impossible.

Whether the appointment was for the right or the wrong reasons, however, was immaterial to Adam Sedgwick. He now had an escape from the drudgery of undergraduate mathematics, and the possibility of an outdoor job that suited his temperament as much as his physical health. The 'active employment' offered by the Woodwardian Chair was the breakthrough he needed. The crisis was resolved; he had an identity, a sense of purpose; equipped with geological hammer, specimen bag and a strong pair of boots, the world lay, literally under his feet. At least he could sleep normally again in a bed.

6

The making of a geologist

In the autumn of 1872, a few months before his death, Adam Sedgwick recalled three things he had hoped to achieve as Woodwardian Professor of Geology:

> First that I might be enabled to bring together—A collection worthy of the University and illustrative of all the departments of the Science it was my duty to teach.
> That a Geological Museum might be built by the University, amply containing its future Collections; and lastly, that I might bring together a class of Students who would listen to my teaching, support me by their sympathy and help me by the labour of their hands. (Sedgwick, 1873)

The geological collection, which was already of importance, was a life-long concern of Sedgwick's and he developed it into a major collection; the Museum was built, but not until after his death and the 'class of students' was brought together for more than half a century. However, all three objectives, in the first instance, depended on Sedgwick's ability to master a relatively new field, in such a way not only to make it a fundamental part of his own knowledge and experience, but to organize it and shape it in a form suitable for teaching to others.

The science of geology in 1818, if not quite 'truly in its infancy', was undergoing a period of unusual development. Although recent research has suggested that in the eighteenth and even in the seventeenth centuries observation of the earth's crust was often remarkably perceptive (Davies, 1969) it wasn't until the last two decades of the eighteenth century that geology began to emerge as a specific scientific discipline. As Roy Porter has observed:

> Before that, study of the earth, through often acute in its theory and accurate in observation, was nevertheless an incoherent jumble of cosmo-

gany, fossil-collecting, Biblical theorizing, topography and so on...
(Porter, 1973)

The word 'geologie' was first used as late as 1778 by J. A. Deluc (1727–1814) in his *Letters Physiques et Morale sur les Montagnes*, when he coined the term for the science that treats the knowledge of the earth which he 'could not venture to adopt ... because it was a word not in use'. Nonetheless, the name caught on, but it was in Freiberg, Saxony that a remarkably charismatic teacher and mineralogist, Abraham Gottlieb Werner (1749–1818) shaped theories of geology that were to dominate the science for nearly half a century. Werner 'a kind of scientific pope' attracted an enormous following and his brilliant lectures inspired enthusiasm and contained much genuine insight (Geikie, 1897: 186). Unfortunately as he had travelled little outside his native Saxony, his elaborate theory of the earth's structure was based on somewhat limited empirical investigations.

This theory, known as Neptunism because it sought to explain the creation of the rocks of the earth entirely through the action of ancient, primeval seas, divided rocks into three major classes:

Primitive Rocks—(the most ancient) these were essentially a result of crystalline chemical precipitations;
Transition Rocks—these were partially chemical and partially sedimentary;
Floetz Rocks—these were produced chiefly by sedimentation.

The most energetic disciple of Werner in Great Britain was Robert Jameson (1774–1854), who from 1804 until his death was Professor of Natural History at Edinburgh University. He founded the Wernerian Natural History Society to help propogate the master's views. Part of the popularity of the Neptunists' views lay with the fact that they could be easily reconciled with a Biblical interpretation of earth history and in particular with the notion of a Noachian Flood; an obsession with many earth scientists in the late eighteenth and early nineteenth century.

However, the Neptunists had important rivals. The most significant of these was a Scottish doctor turned geologist, James Hutton (1726–1797), whose precise and exact observations of the effect of tides and of wind and weather erosion lead him to formulate a view of the earth which saw the slow, constant forces of erosion as being the most significant factor in the evolution of the earth's surface, together with the tremendous effect of heat and fire from within its

The making of a geologist

centre. Unfortunately, the major exposition of his theory, his book *Theory of the Earth* (1795), was difficult and almost unreadable. But his close friend, John Playfair (1748–1819), Professor of Mathematics at Edinburgh, recognizing Hutton's genius, produced a brilliant and lucid account of Hutton's theory, entitled *Illustrations of the Hutton's Theory of the Earth* (1802), which proved immensely influential.

The Huttonians, nicknamed 'Plutonists' because of the emphasis on the action of volcanic forces and fire in their theories gradually gained ascendancy among younger, more radical scholars, but the vast time-scale postulated by the Huttonian 'earth-machine' (Davies, 1969: 150), seemed a direct denial of the Old Testament and godless in its mechanistic view of the Universe. Their most eloquent later disciple was Charles Lyell (1797–1875) whose three volume *Principles of Geology*, published between 1830 and 1833, remains as one of the most influential books in geology. Lyell's insistence on explaining the past as essentially bearing witness to forces that were identical to the present lead to the name 'Uniformitarianism' being given to them by the great Cambridge philosopher of science, and polymath, William Whewell (1794–1866).

Yet many scholars, for scientific as well as religious reasons, failed to fully accept the purely mechanistic Huttonian view and retained a conviction that the clear division between geological eras, particularly as evidenced by the French anatomist and palaeontologist Georges Cuvier (1769–1832), suggested the intervention of periods of sudden cataclysmic changes or upheavals—the shocks and stresses that had perhaps raised the Alps. For this reason, this school of geologists was dubbed by Whewell as 'Catastrophists'. Their most famous advocate in England was the eccentric, charismatic William Buckland (1784–1856), Reader of Geology at Oxford and Dean of Westminster, an entertaining lecturer and celebrated geologist whose famous little blue bag containing an odd fossil or two for an extempore lecture has become part of the folk-lore of geology. For Buckland, the Catastrophic theory could reconcile Geology with Genesis, even if it was necessary to interpret the days of the Biblical Creation in figurative rather than literal terms. His examination of diluvial deposits seemed to provide convincing evidence of the Noachian Flood, and his *Reliquiæ Diluvianæ* of 1823 earned him the description of 'the last British Geologist of note to relate the discovery of modern geology to the Mosaic writings' (Davies, 1969: 215). As someone quipped:

> All was darkness once about the Flood

Adam Sedgwick

Till Buckland rose and made it clear as mud.
(Woodward, 1907: 61)

More significant, perhaps, was the work of Elie de Beaumont on the elevation of mountain chains. Elie de Beaumont (1798–1874) Professor of the Ecole des Mines in Paris, was perhaps the most influential and gifted of the Catastrophists, and although it has been fashionable to see the radical ideas of Hutton, Playfair and Lyell as representing the modern tradition of geological enquiry, the Catastrophists brought important modifications to Uniformitarianism theory so that by the later nineteenth century, geological theory represented more of a blend between the two.

However, it was not learned professors or grand theorists who had the profoundest impact on nineteenth-century geology. It was a West Country canal surveyor of humble origins, William Smith (1769–1839) whose extensive travels in his daily work encouraged him, for the simplest utilitarian reasons, to take careful observations of the landforms through which he was travelling. Smith's career was exactly the type to attract the interest of that indefatigable collector of self-made heroics, Samuel Smiles, and the Victorian classic, *Self Help*, contains a delightful portrait of Smith riding across country, notebook in hand.

> For years he journeyed to and fro, sometimes on foot, sometimes on horseback, riding on the tops of stage coaches, often making up by night travelling the time he had lost by day, so as not to fail in his ordinary business engagements. (Smiles, 1859: 95)

Smith applied to his work a simple, but highly significant, discovery and that was that certain fossils—only recently established by Cuvier, Lamarck and others as remains of extinct species that varied in type and form between strata—were unique to particular strata and, therefore, could be used as reliable evidence for the type—and age of those strata. In other words, as each layer of the earth's sedimentary crust was laid down, the fossil remains of certain species would give a valuable clue to the age, and, therefore, the kind of rocks that would occur in that locality. The benefits of this discovery were enormous. It was immensely useful for a country in the midst of an Industrial Revolution and hungry for raw materials, to have the facility to predict, with some reliability, the mineral wealth or properties of rocks.

William Smith was not slow to see the implications of this. He prepared a superb map entitled *A delineation of the Strata of England and Wales* (1815) and a series of splendid maps of the English

The making of a geologist

counties. It is not without significance that a man involved in creating the network of canals that transformed the English landscape and heralded the Industrial Revolution, should also draw the maps that provided further immense stimulus to that burst of technological growth. But, Smith's great work also opened the way for the development of stratigraphical techniques on a much more sophisticated scale.

> The technique of using fossils invented by William Smith applied by Murchison and Sedgwick and their followers to the study of Welsh rocks opened a way to the unravelling of a very ancient but important phase in the geological history of the world. (Swinnerton, 1960: 49)

It was Sedgwick, indeed, who paid the greatest tribute of all to Smith when, in 1831, as President of of the Geological Society, he presented him with the Society's coveted Wollaston Medal, and described him as 'The Father of English Geology'. Sedgwick's masterly speech on this occasion provides a valuable insight to the effect Smith's work had on his own scientific craft as a geologist:

> I for one can speak with gratitude of the practical lessons I have received from Mr Smith; it was by tracking his footsteps, with his maps in my hand, through Wiltshire and the neighbouring counties where he had trodden nearly thirty years before that I first learnt the subdivisions of our oolitic series, and apprehended the meaning of those arbitrary and somewhat uncouth terms, which we derive from him as our master, which have long become engrafted into the conventional language of the English geologists, and through their influence, have been in part, also adopted by the naturalists of the Continent. (Sedgwick, 1831)

This then was the intellectual background in which the 33-year-old Sedgwick began to master his new craft. He began the pattern of exploratory geology and teaching that was to dominate his entire career from the very first summer of his appointment, spending the vacation among the lead mines of Derbyshire in the Matlock area, before travelling 'on foot with a knapsack' to the copper mines of Staffordshire, looking at the workings, the mineral formations, talking with miners and men who knew the area, and travelling to the salt mines of Cheshire. Invariably, on a geological tour, his health was excellent and the arduous nature of expeditions or uncomfortable nature of quarters were an irrelevance. His ailments only increased as the research had to be written up. On his return to Cambridge, he commenced, in 1819, the first of those annual courses of lectures that distinguished the Cambridge scene almost without interruption for over half a century.

The following Easter he spent some time with a young colleague

Adam Sedgwick

from St John's, J. S. Henslow, on the Isle of Wight. Henslow (1796–1861), later a distinguished naturalist, was to become a lifelong friend. One fruit of that expedition was the germination of an idea for the foundation of a society that was to transform intellectual and scientific life at Cambridge, the Cambridge Philosophical Society. Another was some good geology. It was clear that Sedgwick was, at this time, a Wernerian, regarding the Huttonian thesis as somewhat atheistical. He later recalled being influenced by the Scottish geologist, Dr John McCullouch (1773–1835) 'and saw much from his point of view and was therefore a Wernerian' (Sedgwick, unpublished autobiographical fragment).

In the summer of 1819 he was in Suffolk, then Somerset, Devon and Cornwall; in 1820 it was Dorsetshire, where the rugged cliffs were particularly fascinating. He noted errors in the existing geological maps, and the oolites recorded by Buckland and Conybeare. However, he remained puzzled: 'I did not find it so easy as it had seemed to them'. 1821 was devoted to the chalk wolds and cliffs of East Yorkshire, from Holderness via Flamborough, Scarborough to Whitby—'a dirty stinking town in a very picturesque situation'—and into Durham and Northumberland. These geological tours involved the collection of specimens for the Museum and the careful compilation of material for lectures.

He was now moving away from 'the Wernerian nonsense I learned in my youth' and, in an early paper noted, succinctly, that 'For a long while I was troubled with water on the brain, but light and heat have completely dissipated it', clearly a reference to Plutonians (Clark and Hughes, 1890, vol. I: 285).

In 1822 he was exploring the Pennines. The Yorkshire geologist and topographer, John Phillips (1800–1874), nephew of William Smith, has given a graphic account of a chance first meeting with the new Woodwardian Professor, whose reputation was already growing:

> In the year 1822 I was walking across Durham and North Yorkshire into Westmoreland. It was hot summer-time, and after sketching the High Force, in Teesdale, was reclining in the shade reading some easily carried book. Came riding up, from Middleton, a dark-visaged, conspicuous man, with a miner's boy behind. Opposite me he stopped, and courteously asked if I had looked at the celebrated waterfall which was near; adding that though he had previously visited Teesdale, he had not found an occasion for viewing it; that he would like to stop there and then and do so, but for the boy behind him 'who had him in tow to take him to Cronkley Scar' a high dark hill right ahead, where, he said, 'the limestone was turned into lump-sugar'.

> A few days afterwards, on his way to the lakes, he rested for a few hours at Kirkby Lonsdale to converse with Smith, who was engaged on his geological map of the district, and had just discovered some interesting fossils in the laminated strata below the Old Red Sandstone on Kirkby Moor, perhaps the earliest observation of shells in what afterwards were called Upper Ludlow beds. The two men thus brought together were much different, yet in one respect alike: alike in certain manly simplicity, and unselfish communication of thought. (Phillips, 1873: 98)

However, it was the summer of 1822 that presented Sedgwick with his greatest intellectual challenge. His attention turned to the Lake District, an area of immense geological complexity, whose dramatic, tortured peaks and crags had, since the end of the previous century, attracted poets, novelists, diaryists, topographers and tourists in increasing numbers. So far, these rocks had been dismissed by geologists as 'greywackes' and regarded as a kind of geological no-man's-land.

Hitherto, the only really worthwhile attempt to unravel the statigraphy of the Lakes had been by a local guide and amateur geologist, Jonathan Otley (1766–1856), described by Sedgwick as 'the author of the best guide to the Lakes that was ever written'. During his exploration, Sedgwick met and discussed his work with local enthusiasts. He always generously acknowledged their work and his debt to Otley was considerable. Nonetheless, his elucidation of the complex pattern of ancient Lakeland rocks was a considerable *tour de force* and, for Sedgwick, an important intellectual breakthrough: 'I learned the true lesson of all appearances of the origin of the rocks, often puzzling myself a long time with joints and cleavage plains, ... in that year, 1822, I had learned to distinguish the slanting cleavage from the joints and bedding' (Sedgwick, unpublished autobiographical fragment).

He returned to the Cumbrian mountains in 1823 and 1824, and although it was another seven years before this detailed work was finally formulated into a scholarly paper, 'Introduction to the General Structure of the Cumbrian Mountains' (read in 1831 and published by the Geological Society in 1835), this work formed the basis of some of his most significant geological discoveries.

It was in 1822 that he first met Wordsworth. Their admiration was mutual; their friendship warm and cordial. Though Wordsworth in Book III of *The Excursion* published in 1814, had satirized the new race of geologists chipping away at the Lakeland rocks, he made an exception to his prejudice for Sedgwick. Wordsworth's description of the hurrying geologist is interesting in that it suggests the already

Adam Sedgwick

considerable interest in geology by this time in the Lake District, as the portrait was designed to caricature what must have been a familiar enough figure:

> He who with pocket-hammer smites the edge
> of luckless rock or prominent stone, disguised
> In weather-stains or crusted o'er by Nature,
> With her first growth, detaching by the stroke
> A chip or splinter—to resolve his doubts;
> And, with that ready answer satisfied
> The substance classes by some barbarous name
> And hurries on   (Wordsworth, 1814)

Little record has survived of their meeting and friendship; but it was an active one for Wordsworth was invariably:

> ready for any good occasion that carried him among his well-loved mountains. Hence it was that he joined me in many a lusty excursion, and delighted me (amidst the dry and almost sterile details of my own study, with the outpourings of his manly sense, and with the beautous and healthy images that were ever starting up within his mind during his communion with nature, and were embodied, at the moment, in his own majestic and glowing language.   (Sedgwick, 1853)

It was at this time that Sedgwick promised Wordsworth his 'Letters on the Geology of the Lake District,' perhaps his most famous and widely read work, to accompany Wordsworth's own 'Guide to the Lakes'; a decision he was, curiously, later to regret. John Hudson's *Complete Guide to the Lakes*, which was first published in 1842 and which contained Wordsworth's 'Guide' and Sedgwick's 'Letters' (Sedgwick's old friend Thomas Gough having finally prized the coveted manuscripts from him) owed much of its success to Sedgwick's 'Letters'. Sedgwick was not a little hurt when Jonathan Otley wrote to imply that he felt that his old fellow worker had given Hudson's book a considerable boost. Notwithstanding his friendship with Wordsworth, Sedgwick felt that the excellent Otley should have come first; but he had promised the 'Letters' originally to Wordsworth, and there was no going back. Wordsworth's 'Guide' is, in fact, undoubtedly, a masterpiece in its own right, and Sedgwick's splendid *Letters*, finally increased to five in 1853, remain a classic of geological literature written as they were by the man who had first unravelled the complex Cumbrian rocks.

In later years Sedgwick was a fairly regular visitor to Wordsworth at Rydal Mount when in the Lakes, and during these trips he also met the poet Southey, and, intriguingly, near the summit of Helvellyn, the great chemist and father of atomic theory, John Dalton

(1766–1844), was on one of his annual trips and was armed with a tumbler to measure the dew deposits on the hillside: 'a truth-looking man, of rare simplicity of manners; who, with humble instruments and very humble means, ministered, without flinching, in the service of high philosophy' (Sedgwick, 1853).

Further intellectual stimulus came from Sedgwick's membership of the Geological Society of London—he had been elected a Fellow soon after his appointment to the Woodwardian Chair in 1818. Sedgwick enjoyed the meetings of the Society enormously. It was still a fairly young organization, having been formed

> 'for the purpose of making geologists acquainted with each other, of stimulating their zeal, of industry, of inducing them to adopt one nomenclature, of facilitating the communication of new facts, and of contributing to the advancement of Geological Science, more particularly as connected with the Mineral History of the British Isles. (Woodward, 1907: 18–19)

It would be difficult to overestimate the value of this Society in acting as a focal point for the growth of interest and involvement in the Science, part of the great tradition of energetic individualism and amateurism—in the very best sense of the word—of British science in the early nineteenth century. The published *Transactions* acted as an important disseminator of new information to fellow workers in the field, and allowed the geologist who published new results to acquire a kind of 'property right' to a piece of new knowledge, in the sense of the privilege of giving the name, the nomenclature, to that particular discovery. But, according to Sedgwick, it was also a gathering of:

> robust, joyous and independent spirits, who toiled well in the field, and also did battle and cuffed opinions with much spirit and great good will. For they had one great object before them, the promotion of true knowledge; and not one of them was deeply committed to any system of opinions. (Sedgwick, 1873)

Sedgwick, with his immense energy, enthusiasm and lively personality, quickly established himself as a leading member of the Society; he was a member of Council by 1824, by 1827 a Vice President, and by 1829 its President.

From about this period, Sedgwick's first major scientific contribution, based on work done five or six years earlier, appeared in the paper 'On the Magnesian Limestone and Lower Portions of the New Red Sandstone Series', which was read to the Society at intervals between 1826 and 1828, and examined the broad terrain of Mag-

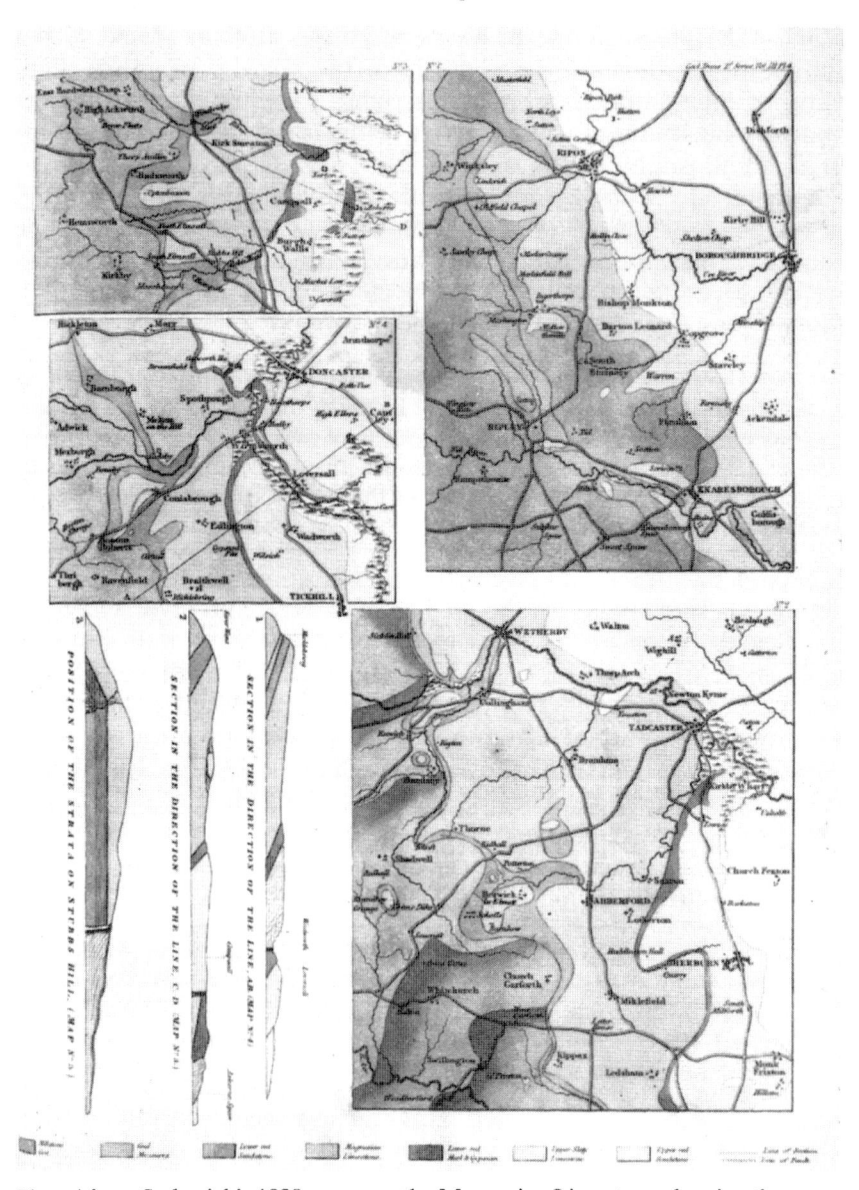

Plate 4 from Sedgwick's 1829 paper on the Magnesian Limestone showing the range of the formation in Yorkshire.

nesian Limestone which stretches across England from the Midlands to the Tyne and its relationship with the new Red Sandstone. This classic analysis remains a standard interpretation of the phenomenon.

The making of a geologist

Among many of the bright young intellectuals drawn to the Geological Society was a young Scot, a veteran of the Peninsular War, who, having inherited a Highland Estate that had been sold for the princely fortune of £27,000, had devoted his considerable energies to fox-hunting and a gay social life. He was Roderick Impey Murchinson (1792–1871). His wife Charlotte Hugonin 'attractive, piquant, clever, highly educated', and a keen naturalist in her own right, realized her husband was in some danger of dissipating his not inconsiderable abilities in mere hedonistic frivolities. She therefore developed an interest in palaeontology and geology in her husband to such good effect that Murchison became a member of the Geological Society and immediately became drawn by Sedgwick's personality.

> From his buoyant and cheerful nature, as well as from his soul and eloquence, Sedgwick at once won my heart, and a year only was to elapse before we became co-adjutors in a survey of the Highlands and afterwards of various parts of the Continent. (Geikie, 1875, vol. I: 125)

The Highland trip in 1827 was a huge success; in spite of a considerable difference in background and personality the relationship between the two men developed into an exciting creative partnership. From the outset, Sedgwick was the teacher, brilliantly expounding basic principles:

> Under Sedgwick's guidance he [Murchison] saw clearly enough the meaning of things which has puzzled him not a little before. For example, even at that early time, Sedgwick had distinguished that peculiar structure in rock to which the name 'cleavage' is now given, and taught his companion to recognise it. (Geikie, 1875, vol. I: 139)

Something of the huge sense of fun, of the vitality of the explorers in what was still a fairly remote territory, can be gathered from Geikie's account of the trip:

> with Sedgwick in the party the tour could not possibly be all work and no play. They threw themselves heartily into the ways of the Highlanders, and made friends all along the route—ate haggis and drank whisky at one house, danced in rough coats and hobnailed boots in another, brightened with talk the dining room of a third. (Geikie, 1875, vol. I: 140)

On another occasion between Greenock and Ullapool Sedgwick had to bale out with his hat the leaking boat they were travelling in and elsewhere they were 'mistaken for a couple of drovers and got but scant courtesy!'

The difference in the financial circumstances between the two men can be encapsulated in the fact that in 1822 Murchison had contributed £50 as an annual subscription to a pack of foxhounds. That was exactly half the Woodwardian Professor's total income in 1820, which had been increased subsequently to £200 per annum, only as a result of a well argued plea to the Vice Chancellor of the University and Heads of Colleges.

Sedgwick's pupil moreover, was not saddled with the need to earn his living by the increasingly demanding round of College and academic duties. Sedgwick was, for example, appointed a Senior Proctor soon after his return from the Highland trip, and had to spend time that might otherwise have been devoted to the important task of preparing the paper on the geology of Arran and on the old Red Sandstone of Scotland that he and Murchison were due to give, subduing drunken or dissipated undergraduates or discovering 'evildoers *Flagrante delicto* and having them removed from the University' (Clark and Hughes, 1890, vol I: 308).

Sedgwick's colleague at Trinity, the brilliant mathematician Charles Babbage (1792–1871), in his *Reflection on the Decline of Science in England* published in 1830, noted that 'it appears that scarcely any man can be expected to pursue abstract science unless he possess a private fortune, and unless he can resolve to give up all intentions of improving it'. And the few (like Sedgwick) fortunate enough to obtain an academic post in science would find that 'while the salaries attached are seldom sufficient for the sole support of an individual, they are rarely enough for that of a family' (Babbage, 1830: 38).

Murchinson, then, had many of the things that Sedgwick lacked—wealth, leisure and a loving wife whom he could either take with him on Continental travels or leave at home in quiet domesticity. He also had splendid health, immense energy (he once for the sport of it, walked 452 miles in 14 days, or on another occasion, performed the 'pedestrian feat' of walking 120 miles to Mont Blanc in three days) and blazing ambition. Perhaps this was a clue to the success of their partnership; Sedgwick, the more senior and more capable geologist, weighed down by College duties, urged on by the energetic, ambitious and even impetuous Murchison. Frequently Murchison had to urge his friend to action over writing up their joint researches. Eventually two joint papers were completed and duly given with some success to the Geological Society.

In the summer of 1829 the two friends set out on a Continental Tour to the Alps, crossing the Tyrol to Italy, meeting up with the liberal Archduke John and accompanying him on a trip to the Carinthian glacier, everywhere enjoying a reception which mingled

The making of a geologist

Sir Roderick Impey Murchison (1792–1871).

something of an aristocratic Grand Tour and a scientific expedition, meeting local geologists, travelling across the mountains on foot or by carriage. In Trieste Murchison noted how his companion could gorge 'good ice and water melons that would make any man ill except Sedgwick' (Geikie, 1875, vol. I: 159)—hardly the hypochondriac who so often complained about the problems of his digestive system. Ultimately, the trip produced more useful papers, which were presented to the Geological Society in the autumn of that same year.

In 1830 they separated, Sedgwick working in Yorkshire, doing some excellent work in the Pennines, elucidating the complex faulting system that separated the Carboniferous rocks of the Yorkshire Dales from the systems of the Lake District, and examining the New Red Sandstone systems around the Vale of Eden and the Cumbrian Coast.

However, it was the fiendishly complex rock systems of Wales that next attracted both Sedgwick and Murchison. In 1831 Murchison chose to begin the difficult task of unravelling the so-called 'Transition Rocks' or in Murchison's phrase 'interminable greywacke' in the South-east of the Principality, whilst Sedgwick began work among the even more confused and complex ancient rocks of the North.

Murchison worked in Shropshire and Herefordshire, and was delighted to discover that a number of local amateur geologists had already done a great deal of unpublished work in the area and he was able to make excellent progress; interestingly enough, Thomas Lewis, the most gifted of these amateurs, had attended Sedgwick's lectures whilst at Cambridge, and, on taking up his clerical duties at Aymestry and inspired by Sedgwick, began elucidating the local strata and by 1829 had already traced out what later was to be recognized as the Upper Silurian system in the area.

> Although at one time he thought of publishing the geology, yet, when he made acquaintance with Murchison, he cheerfully resigned the subject, rejoicing that it had fallen into the hands of a geologist whose practical knowledge was much greater than his own. (Woodward, 1907: 94)

In the meantime Sedgwick was at work in Caernarvonshire, Merioneth, Montgomery and Denbighshire, and soon noted similarities between the slates of North Wales and Cumberland; the work was difficult, even baffling. He returned again in 1832 and yet again in 1834, and although many difficulties still lay ahead, his grasp on the essence of the structures of the tortured, distorted, dislocated layers of rock was astounding. It was as if, in his greatest work, Sedgwick was able to combine a Dawsonian mathematical training with the skill of a field-geologist in order to penetrate, unravel and explain reality as he perceived it; this was empirical science of the very highest order.

As Clark and Hughes claim (and there seems little reason to modify this view) by 1832 Sedgwick had:

> explained the geological structure of North Wales; had sketched the leading subdivision of the Cambrian rocks; had established the correct sequence of the Arenig and Bala—series, and had placed them in true relation with what were afterwards known as Silurian. (Clark and Hughes, 1890: 523–4)

In 1835, after having worked together in South Wales, Murchison and Sedgwick chose the British Association meeting in Dublin to present a joint paper 'On the Silurian and Cambrian Systems, exhibiting the order in which the older Sedimentary Strata succeed each other in England and Wales.' This event was an important one. Murchison had chosen the name 'Silurian' after an ancient British tribe for the Upper System of rocks his researches had described; spurred into action Sedgwick chose the name 'Cambrian' also after a Welsh tribe to describe the Lower systems. Fossil and other evidence indicated that these were truly different geological systems, and although neither geologist, at this date, could establish the exact point of difference between the two, the decision to publish a joint paper indicated at this date the willingness of the two 'fellow-labourers' to respect each other's unwritten territorial right. For the first time, the older or Palaeozoic rocks, not only of the British Isles, but of the world, were unlocked. Murchison, in particular, was quick to realize the implications: 'His domain of "Siluria" became in his eyes a kind of personal property over which he watched with solicitude' (Geikie, 1875, vol. I: 243).

As early as 1832 Sedgwick became aware of the difficulty of establishing, clearly, the point of division between the Upper Cambrian and Lower Silurian systems; noting an area of apparent overlap, he wrote to Murchison: 'Don't suppose I want to steal that mountain from you, I only mean that our sections must overlap and so much the better'. At the time, perhaps tragically, the differences did not seem significant enough to pursue. There seemed no reason why there should not be a rational means of establishing the exact dividing point between the two systems.

By 1835 Sedgwick was at the height of his creative power. His paper of that year 'Remarks on the Structure of Large Mineral Masses' opened up an exciting new area of research on the effects of heat and enormous pressure on strata; he had, through his empirical work, given other geologists an immensely valuable insight into the most difficult of the world's remaining unexplored rock systems. As Professor Rudwick (1975) suggests, 'his exposition of the distinction between stratification, jointing and slaty cleavage provided the crucial technical key for the interpretation of regions with complex folding'.

Inevitably his most spectacular achievement in the eyes of the geological world was the establishment of the Cambrian system. It was, and remains, a 'discovery' in the classic sense, and one with which Sedgwick's name was, and always will be, associated. For a scholar of limited means, like Sedgwick, this must inevitably have generated a curious sense of achievement, of fulfillment. Yet the irony was that the Cambrian system, which brought all these things,

Adam Sedgwick

Adam Sedgwick, aged 47

was also to be the source of his most bitter disillusionment, frustration and sense of betrayal.

However, for Sedgwick there was always that other dimension, Dent. During vacations, sometimes in between extended field trips and the start of the University year, he would return to his now extended family. After the death of his parents, his family centred around 'his brothers and sisters and a growing number of nephews and nieces'. His younger brother, John, having succeeded his father as Vicar of Dent, kept the Old Parsonage in the family and Adam had inherited a little property in the valley. Travel was still agonizingly slow—railways were only just beginning to be built, and never penetrated Dentdale in Sedgwick's lifetime—and a letter to Murchison in 1836 gives a vivid and entertaining account of the difficulties of travel across the remote and lonely mountain pass from Kirkby Lonsdale to Dent over Barbondale, during a typical Dentdale blizzard.

The making of a geologist

My adventures during the last stage before I reached Dent were laughable enough. I took a post-chaise from Kirkby-Lonsdale and was deluded to attempt the high, rugged mountain road; but it was so dark and misty, accompanied with sleet and wind, that the driver twice got off the road, and the post-chaise was once on its side, though easily righted. This I did not like, so I mounted by the side of my Jehu, and before ten minutes were over we again missed the road, and were within an ace of rolling neck and crop into a hollow made by one of the mountain streams. With some difficulty we got the horses again into the old wheel-tracks, for there was hardly the appearance of a formed road. I took out one of the lamps, and walked for seven miles with a hairy cap on my head and a boa about my neck, all bespattered with sleet and snow, and looking like an old grizzly watchman. The driver following my light, and I lead him safely to the top of the pass which overhangs my native valley. All's well that ends well. My friends gave me a hearty welcome and a blazing fire.
(Clark and Hughes, 1890, vol. II: 455–6)

But even this road, the road he used to return home so often between Cambridge and Dent, as the years went by, was to have an increasingly melancholy significance. So often he was recalled to Dent in tragic circumstances, the death of his parents, of his beloved sister Isabella, of Margaret. It was on the occasion of Margaret's death in 1856 that the full significance to him of the beautiful Barbondale pass was all too apparent:

We [Adam Sedgwick and his brother John] went together up the beautiful valley of the Lune, and over the high wild pass which leads to Dent, almost in silence. The country had no charms for me, as my mind was filled with other images, and shadows of former thoughts. I came up this pass in 1820 in the hope of seeing my dying mother, but was too late to look on her living face. This was my first great domestic sorrow. Again, in 1823, I forced my way through this pass on foot, after trying in vain on horseback. Before I had made my way through the great snowdrifts that crossed the pass I met a countryman and a shepherd who told me that my beloved sister, the companion of my childhood was dead. I hoped to have received her parting blessing, and to have comforted her; but this happiness was denied me. In 1828 I crossed the same mountains to my father's funeral, but I knew of the old man's death before I started.   (Clark and Hughes, 1890, vol. II: 313–14)

7

Controversy I: Cambrian versus Silurian

In November 1834, on the day before he resigned as Lord Chancellor, the Whig peer, Lord Brougham, heard of the death of one of the Canons of Norwich Cathedral and anxious to assist a prominent Liberal like Sedgwick, he offered him the living. It was a Prebendaryship, one of six of Norwich, each holder of which resided in Norwich for two months of the year. Sedgwick's allocation was from December 1st to January 31st and he would thus be able to continue his professorial duties at Cambridge.

It offered an income of £600 a year for the duties, three times his Woodwardian salary. Sedgwick seized the opportunity gladly, as it meant an unimagined degree of financial security, but he was soon to realize the position was no sinecure. During those two months there was an incessant round of duties, including the long services that he noted 'cut my time to shreds and destroy the spirit of labour'. Norwich, however welcome its income, was a further drain on his mental and physical resources. Because he was of a conscientious disposition, the duties absorbed an increasing amount of his energies (Clark and Hughes, 1890, vol. II: 465–6). It also meant that College duties had to be compressed into the remaining months.

Even though there might be less time for field geology, when Henry De la Beche (1796–1855), an enthusiastic geologist who had persuaded the Board of Ordnance to sponsor his geological map of the county of Devon, reported that he had discovered fossil plants presumably belonging to the Carboniferous period under the 'greywacke' rocks, Sedgwick was alarmed. He felt that the matter was important enough to accompany Murchison, in the summer of 1836, to North Devon. Predictably, the 'true position' of the puzzling Culm Measures was soon established as Carboniferous rocks lying above Greywacke.

Controversy I: Cambrian versus Silurian

This would, of course, create a difficulty in that it would involve a formal contradiction of De la Beche's work. Only in 1835 Sedgwick, Buckland and Lyell had presented a joint report to the Master-General and Board of Ordnance which lead to the establishment of the Geological Survey and to the appointment of De la Beche as its first director. De la Beche was a capable field geologist and Murchison was anxious, not without reason, about the reception De la Beche would give to their joint paper, due to be delivered to the Geological Society that Autumn. Sedgwick, as usual, was behind with his promised material for Murchison, since he was under considerable pressure of work at this time. A bout of influenza prevented him completing a final draft, and only a somewhat muddled letter arrived for the distraught Murchison, about to meet a hostile audience alone. The paper was deferred. When it was given at a later meeting it created a lively debate (Sedgwick and Murchison, 1839), But it was clear that many questions about these ancient rocks remained unanswered. The fossil evidence in the rocks seemed to suggest Silurian, but the rock types were different. Could they be Cambrian?

It was about this time that William Lonsdale (1794–1871) a gifted palaeontologist, suggested that the fossils of North Devon had similarities with those of the Old Red Sandstone of Scotland. Sedgwick and Murchison sent further samples to Lonsdale and others realizing that they had been misinformed about earlier specimens. Further observations confirmed Lonsdale's view; the truth could only be explained by establishing a separate rock system of an era between Silurian and Carboniferous, of which the Old Red Sandstone was a part. Their historic paper, 'Classification of the Older Stratified Rocks of Devonshire and Cornwall', was read to the Geological Society in March 1839, and subsequently established the great system known as the Devonian: 'undoubtedly the greatest change which has ever been attempted at one time in the classification of British Rocks' (Geikie, 1897: 432).

However, it was more than a question of British rocks, in the summer and early autumn of 1839 Sedgwick and Murchison convincingly demonstrated to sceptical continental geologists that the Devonian system was in evidence in Germany. This trip to the Rhineland and Harz Mountains again evidenced Sedgwick in the best of spirits. As Murchison recounted in a letter to his wife, 'Sedgwick is as well as I ever knew him—eats, drinks and digests like a Hercules, and is in great force' (Geikie, 1875, vol. I: 276). Only a few months earlier, between Cambridge and Norwich with the preparation of the Devonian papers for the press, he is reported to have

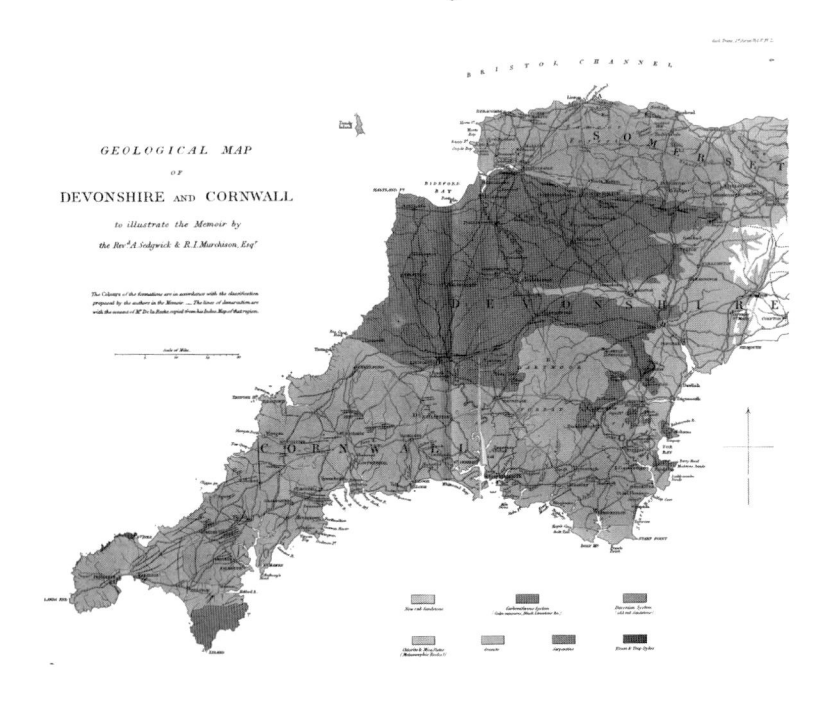

Plate 50 from Sedgwick's and Murchison's (1840) classic paper on the physical structure of Devonshire.

been suffering from gout, mental prostration and loss of intellect. (Clark and Hughes, 1890, vol. I: 524).

Yet again, therefore, Sedgwick and Murchison had established a world-system, and their nomenclature remains. They had, in fact, only beaten fellow-workers in the United States by a few months and had the usual Sedgwickian procrastination continued for only a short while longer, the 'Devonian' system would have been known as 'Erian' (Wells, 1938: 56).

Early in 1839, too, Murchison published his great *Silurian System*, dedicated to Sedgwick, a massive two-volume, 820 page *magnum opus*, which was intended to establish its author's reputation as the King of Siluria. With its wealth of detail, its excellent illustrations and its vitality, it did just that. Much as Sedgwick admired the work, it is impossible to believe that it would not serve to remind him of his own failure to produce a similar grand work. Over the years previously he had planned to produce with W. D. Conybeare a sequel to the latter's *Outlines of the Geology of England and Wales*, written with W. Phillips and published in 1822. Because of pressure of work and other factors it was never written.

Controversy I: Cambrian versus Silurian

THE

SILURIAN SYSTEM,

FOUNDED ON

GEOLOGICAL RESEARCHES

IN THE COUNTIES OF

SALOP, HEREFORD, RADNOR, MONTGOMERY, CAERMARTHEN, BRECON, PEMBROKE, MONMOUTH, GLOUCESTER, WORCESTER, AND STAFFORD;

WITH
DESCRIPTIONS OF THE COAL-FIELDS AND OVERLYING FORMATIONS.

BY

RODERICK IMPEY MURCHISON, F.R.S. F.L.S.

VICE-PRESIDENT OF THE GEOLOGICAL SOCIETY OF LONDON,
GENERAL SEC. BRIT. ASSOC. ADVANCEMENT OF SCIENCE,
MEMBER OF THE ROYAL GEOGRAPHICAL SOCIETY,
HON. MEM. OF THE ROYAL IRISH ACADEMY,
ETC. ETC. ETC.

IN TWO PARTS.

PART I.

LONDON:
JOHN MURRAY, ALBEMARLE STREET.
1839.

Title page of Murchison's *magnum opus*, 1839.

However, *The Silurian System* also brought into the open certain disagreements between Sedgwick and Murchison over that vexed problem of the exact difference between Cambrian and Silurian systems. Murchison had, indeed, consulted his friend in the preparation of the book and it was clear that areas considered by Sedgwick to consist of Cambrian rocks were being classified as Silurian by Murchison. This 'encroachment', Sedgwick confessed, 'left in my mind a feeling not of anger but of sorrow, mingled with a most wretched and miserable condition of surprise, uncertainty and suspicion.'

The origin of the conflict—which was to develop into one of the major geological controversies of the century—lay, initially, in a simple, but fundamental, error on the part of Murchison. He had misinterpreted the age of certain rocks around the areas of Llandeilo and Caradoc in the Welsh borders and consequently assumed that these rocks must form the base line of the Lower Silurian system, rather than, as in Sedgwick's view, the Upper part of the Cambrian. Initially, Sedgwick had accepted Murchison's interpretation of these areas, but this interpretation raised difficult and awkward problems, which seemed to contradict this finding. Sedgwick's own Bala Beds were similar in many respects to the Caradoc Beds of Murchison, but the former were described by Sedgwick as Cambrian, the latter Silurian by Murchison. Sooner or later the difference would have to be resolved.

The differences went deeper than this. Sedgwick, who went as far as to confess, in his 'autobiographical fragment', that although he knew fossils 'by sight' he did not always know them by name, insisted that in field analysis, palaeontology, (or the study of fossils) should be subservient to lithology (or the recognition of the mineral or other properties of strata). In 1831 Sedgwick stated his position forcefully:

> Through large regions of the earth, the epoch of many deposits is not less defined by the mineral content of the rocks, than by their organised contents. Accurate mineralogical distinctions, and an order of superposition determined by natural sections is the first foundation of the geology of every country. Organic remains often help us to associate disconnected base lines. They also help us to subdivide the successive deposits of an epoch, in areas where all other means fail; and in speculating on the former condition of the earth they are invaluable; but they can in no instance supercede the necessity of study in detail of the structure and superposition of the great mineral masses covering the surface of the globe. (Sedgwick, 1831)

But as Rudwick has demonstrated, Murchison increasingly defined his Silurian 'system' in terms of its distinctive fauna, and in particular was anxious to include, as part of his 'stratigraphical imperialism', all rocks containing what appeared to be the first manifestations of life on the planet, going to the extent of including among the 'Lower Silurian' a quite distinctive primeval fauna noted by the French palaeontologist Barrande (1799–1883) even though it did not match any known Silurian fossil specimen. Whereas Sedgwick anticipated a degree of overlap or gradualism in fossil evidence, Murchison used such evidence to include the Upper Cambrian into his own Silurian. Even on his own terms his inclusion of Barrande's primeval fossils went wrong—but it was necessary to fulfil a peculiar kind of intellectual ambition:

> When Barrande discovered in Bohemia a new and distinctive 'Primordial' fauna (the Cambrian of modern geology) lying below all that had hitherto been termed 'Silurian', Murchison at once annexed this too to his 'Lower Silurian', despite the fact that it was quite distinct in palaeontological character. Murchison was therefore not consistent even with his own theoretical commitment. (Rudwick, 1976; 375)

And clearly, the notion that the Silurian included the beginning of life on the planet could, for Murchison, strike a chord in the grand manner: 'How clearly do we read in the book of nature opened out in the north of continental Europe that Silurian fossils constitute the earliest recognisable creation' (Murchison, 1839).

It was in order to resolve these major contradictions that, in 1843, Sedgwick returned to re-examine his sections in North Wales, this time taking with him a gifted young palaeontologist, J. W. Salter (1820–1869).

Sedgwick has left us a detailed account of the trip, and their method of work: 'we spent many a merry day together—most of the day, and every evening, while I slept on the sofa, Salter made the notes, labelled the fossils, made the tea, and woke me up in time to go to bed. I rose at 5' (Sedgwick, unpublished MS.).

There is also an entertaining description of how their horses escaped on one occasion, with all their specimens, but were recaptured, and 'giving them their head' they galloped back to base. But the real purpose of the expedition was to seek the truth', and Sedgwick claimed 'we would have embraced it, to whatever conclusions it might lead us' (Sedgwick, unpublished MS.).

It led to confirmation of Sedgwick's earlier work, a fact later further reinforced by the Geological Survey of Great Britain. In contrast when they visited South Wales, a certain amount of Murchison's work required major revision. As a field-geologist Murchison was not, unfortunately, of the same calibre as Sedgwick.

But by now Murchison was seeking new horizons. He was travelling (in 1841) in Russia and was a guest of Tsar Nicolas I, returning again in 1845 to visit the Ural Mountains. He received a knighthood from Queen Victoria in 1846 and was honoured by the Tsar for his services to Russian geology shortly afterwards. His fame and influence were growing—he was popular, elegant and stylish, and he had the satisfaction of seeing his nomenclature increasingly adopted by geologists around the world.

To alter this nomenclature would have been to lose face; his position would have been threatened, his dignity disturbed. Moreover, the fossil evidence seemed to support what he had said and he was not going to jeopardize his reputation over a trivial question of nomenclature. What was the point if others were also accepting it? He admitted too, that he had published in haste in order to secure that vitally important credit of discovery: 'But I am told by Logan and others *that if I had delayed a single year or two* in bringing out my Silurian system with all its fossils the Yankees would have anticipated me. And you well know that Wales, North and South, was not to be puzzled out in less than many years of hard labour' (Clark and Hughes, 1890, Vol. II: 219).

Sedgwick, whatever his feelings, maintained cordial relationships with his old fellow-labourer even though he was saddened that his suggested use of the term 'Protozoic' for Cambro-Silurian rocks as a means of avoiding needless controversy was rejected by Murchison. But events came to a head in 1852 when the Geological Survey published the Map of North Wales which used Murchison's nomenclature for large areas of Sedgwick's Cambrian. Sedgwick was furious. It was a crushing, personal insult, being achieved, as Sedgwick saw it by a backdoor method. Though realising it had been probably his fault through not publishing his own work, nonetheless he saw it as a personal betrayal:

> Still, though a man is behind time with his rent, he rather grumbles when he finds, on coming back to his premises that a neighbour has turned out his furniture, taken possession, and locked the door upon him. This was exactly what you did; and so completely, unexpectedly and without notice, that the first time I ever heard of your having Silurianized the Map of Wales was from that parasitic geologist Knipe. (Clark and Hughes, 1890, vol II: 251)

Sedgwick's public response was to present a paper to the Geological Society entitled 'On the Classification and Nomenclature of the Lower Palaeozoic Rocks of England and Wales' which, as well as presenting a detailed account of his researches in the Lake District and North Wales, claimed the 'right of naming the Cambrian groups because I flinched not from their difficulties, made out their general structure, collected their fossils, and first comprehended their respective relations to the groups above them and below them, in the great and complicated Palaeozoic sections of North Wales' (Sedgwick, 1852).

Controversy I: Cambrian versus Silurian

However, as Woodward later recorded: 'it may be candidly stated that it did contain some passages that tended to impugn the good faith of Murchison' (Woodward, 1907: 180–1) The Council considered the paper with care and tactfully decided to publish 'in an abstracted form as recommended by the Referee' who was none other than admirable John Phillips. However, through some internal mix-up, the full paper was published and caused consternation. Foolishly the Council tried to 'recall the journal' and cancel pages '152 to the end'. Not surprisingly Sedgwick saw this as a crude attempt at censorship; the controversy was intensified.

In spite of the dispute the two continued to correspond, and, at least in correspondence kept up the semblance of their old comradeship—at the end of a long letter to Murchison hammering away at the question of the true nature of the Caradoc Beds, he could finish as 'your affectionate old friend'.

In September 1833, accompanied by his pupil Frederick McCoy (1823–1899), Sedgwick went down to May Hill near the Forest of Dean to examine these Caradoc rocks, and with for him astonishing speed, by November presented his paper 'On the Separation of the so called Caradoc Sandstone' to the Geological Society; it occasioned considerable controversy and was only printed after some debate, particularly as Sedgwick had been forbidden by the Society 'to bring before them any paper involving the Classification and Nomenclature of our older Palaeozoic rocks' (Woodward, 1907: 184).

This was further developed in a paper first given to the Geological Society in May 1854 and entitled 'On the May Hill Sandstone and the Palaeozoic System of England'. The significance of this paper was that it confirmed the fundamental error that lay at the basis of Murchison's annexation of the Upper Cambrian. As Rudwick suggests, Murchison

> had misinterpreted the Lower Silurian succession in its type area and had therefore believed that the strata were younger than the Upper Cambrian when in fact they were the same age and—an even more serious mistake—he had wrongly incorporated some Upper Silurian strata (May Hill Sandstone) into the Lower Silurian, Caradoc Series, despite their very different fauna, thus giving the Silurian faunas a spurious uniformity down to Sedgwick's Cambrian.   (Rudwick, 1975: 584)

However, the Geological Society, not surprisingly, terrified by the implication of the paper and the intensity of the controversy, demanded changes; Sedgwick took umbrage, withdrew the paper and published it in the *Philosophical Magazine*, and did not again ever attend a meeting of the Society. The paper forced the Society to re-examine the Caradoc area and Sedgwick was vindicated, but the nomenclature was not changed in the way that he had hoped, and the deeper implications were ignored. As Thackray argues, for Sedgwick 'to see Murchison's classification accepted in spite of such a blunder must have been hard to bear' (Thackray, 1976).

By now, the Cambro-Silurian controversy was a national issue, with geologists split into opposing camps, the establishment by and large being on Murchison's side. After the death of De la Beche in 1855 Murchison was appointed Director General of the Geological Survey which now included the Geological Museum and School of Mining. He could now ensure, from a position of immense prestige and influence, that his nomenclature was safeguarded, would be increasingly recognized and accepted by younger men, and defended by a powerful bureaucratic mechanism.

Nonetheless, the estrangement from Sedgwick hurt him deeply. Ironically, in the same year that the paper 'On the May Hill Sandstone' was published Murchison published his *Siluria*, a substantial sequel to *The Silurian System*. The copy of the book sent to Sedgwick, and still kept in the Sedgwick Museum, is inscribed 'To Professor Sedgwick from his old fellow labourer'.

At first, the cordial relationship continued at least on the surface. The conflict was purely intellectual. At the British Association in Glasgow in 1855, when Sedgwick rose to speak on a paper given by Murchison and deliberately took off his great-coat, he could still delight his audience by quipping 'Oh I'm not going to fight him' (Clark and Hughes, 1890, vol. II: 304).

By the 1860s, the gap was real indeed. Both men were, to some extent, to blame. In his old age, wracked by gout, loneliness and a sense of frustration at what he saw as an inability of the geological establishment to understand the significance of his May Hill paper, and, most of all, disturbed by the realization that his life's great work was not going to be written, Sedgwick was an embittered man. Murchison too, was in no position to yield in the crucial question of the Caradoc beds, realizing that this would cause questions to be asked about the whole of his interpretation of the Silurian: 'If I give up the Llandeilo, and part of the Caradoc, what will be left of my Silurian?'.

What particularly angered Sedgwick was the fact that, as he had not questioned his friend's work in the 1830s and had altered his own work to be in 'supposed accordance' with Murchison, Murchison now implied the errors were his (Clark and Hughes, 1890, vol. II:

Controversy I: Cambrian versus Silurian

543–4). So, when Lady Affleck in 1859 sought to achieve a reconciliation between the two celebrated geological opponents, she must have been not a little unnerved at the violence of Sedgwick's response: 'I cannot meet Sir Roderick Murchison as a friend till he retracts, before the Geological Society, publically and formally, a statement which he made in their printed journal'.

He went on to accuse Murchison of 'one of the greatest and most mischievous blunders in the history of English geology a direct and deliberate untruth', and to admit that he would have quit the Geological Society if he could have overcome his feelings for a Society 'for which I had for so many a long year been a hard working member and in which I had made so many trusted friends'. Murchison had been 'false in word and deed' (Sedgwick, 1862).

This same violent reaction was manifest in a rebuff to Murchison as late as 1868, when at the age of 83, Sedgwick was still unrepentant. The correspondence hurt Murchison so deeply that he instructed his executors to print it only if further untruths were written about him and it is omitted from Geikie's biography. Sedgwick's accusation is severe:

> When without a single word of explanation ... before the Geological Society you spread your Silurian colour over those parts of North Wales which I had laboriously and successfully examined, and allowed your fellow labourer to pick up this knowledge more than two years afterwards from an itinerant map seller, I bore the contemptuous insult with patience.
>
> But when (at a subsequent period) you dared to affirm that in the great mistakes you had made in interpreting the order of superposition among the older groups of North and South Wales, you had been misled by myself, I could no longer regard you as my personal friend, or as one in whom I could repose any confidence.
>
> I remain no longer your intimate and affectionate friend as I once was, but still your well wisher as a Christian Brother though now a stranger to you.   (Sedgwick, 1869a)

Murchison was deeply grieved, particularly no doubt from feelings of guilt at the wrong done to his old friend. A letter, which was never sent, states that 'the rupture of our former friendship has always been felt by me as one of the greatest misfortunes which ever befell me' (Murchison, 1869a).

But he finally actually wrote 'it would make me 'young again' as well as yourself and would give me the most satisfaction of any explanation which I can possibly give you would be accepted by you, and would put an end to the estrangement which for more than 20 years I have never ceased to lament' (Murchison, 1869b).

However, Sedgwick's reply was brutal:

> Your nomenclature of the older English rocks is false for the simple reason that below your true Silurian groups (beginning with Wenlock Shale) your original and typical section and your order of superposition are false. My order of superposition was not false in any essential part ... you have acted contemptuously, unjustly and falsely towards me. I cannot smooth over the matter by the shallow gloss of vulgar courtesy or by the abuse of the name of friendship. As a brother worker I have rejoiced in your success, and still in the feebleness of old age I can scarcely wish you ill or harm through the remnant of your life.   (Sedgwick, 1869c)

By then it was too late, Murchison was in no position to sacrifice his reputation.

The violence of Sedgwick's language reflects a deep inner disappointment. His greatest achievement, as an empirical scientist, lay in his brilliant unravelling of the ancient rocks of North Wales. The May Hill papers, written against the tide of current opinion, had taken the ground away, literally, from under Murchison's feet. According to everything that was right and just, he should have achieved not mere personal recognition, but the establishment of a hard won truth.

But the clear water of science was muddied by political and personal connivance. Murchison had become a symbol of that betrayal. It was mingled too, with a recognition that a man, who, when everything else was said, was his inferior in the essential geologist's craft, had achieved world wide recognition, the accolade of two major contributions to geological literature and appointment as Knight Commander of the Bath. To a man with essential simplicity and purity of vision of Sedgwick, Sir Roderick Impey Murchison's edifice of fame was founded on a lie.

Yet when Murchison's wife Charlotte, died in February 1869, a flood of compassion overcame him. He wrote with great difficulty because of the eye trouble that plagued him, but with the old tenderness:

> For many years Lady Murchison was one of the dearest of those friends whose society formed the best charms of my life. How often was I her guest! How often have I experienced her kind welcome, and been strengthened by it ... I generally dictate my long letters to my servant, but in writing this letter of sympathy, addressed to you in your hour of sorrow, I could not find it in my heart to use the pen of an amanuensis. My eyes are now very angry. I remain, in all Christian sympathy and goodwill, faithfully yours. Adam Sedgwick.   (Sedgwick, 1869d)

Controversy I: Cambrian versus Silurian

This was the last letter they ever exchanged.

Ironically, Sedgwick never did receive full recognition of his work. In 1879, Charles Lapworth's brilliant study of graptolites, minute pencil-like organisms, suggested that the Upper Cambrian of Sedgwick and the Lower Silurian of Murchison formed a further distinct series to themselves, which he duly named 'Ordovician' after the Ordovices, an ancient tribe of central Wales. The geological maps were redrawn, much of Sedgwick's Cambrian reclaimed and the Silurian reduced to a more modest geological band. Sir Roderick would have been deeply offended, but Adam Sedgwick, if a little hurt, would have felt quietly vindicated.

8

I can only fire your imagination

The first course of lectures Sedgwick gave to his students at Cambridge took place in 1819; he continued to give an annual course, almost uninterrupted, until 1870. Rather charmingly, each series was given its appropriate number—'I am delivering my 40th course' or whatever the year (Clark and Hughes, 1890, vol. I: 203), until his fifty-second at the remarkable age of 85. Because the lectures were in no way compulsory, nor even, until the establishment of the Natural Science Tripos in 1848, related in any way to the examination system, undergraduates could attend Sedgwick's lectures purely as the interest took them. They were also 'public' in the sense that anyone in the town who wished could, and often did, attend.

Evidence suggests that Sedgwick's lectures were extraordinarily good, both from the quality of their content, and the remarkable technical skill of the lecturer. Some notion of the content can be grasped from the successive *Syllabi* of courses of lectures, which were first published in 1821 and reviewed constantly. The syllabus outlined the lectures and presented a brief synopsis, which was intended to inform students of the contents of the course and serve as a structure for the lecture.

His method of preparing a lecture was to paste a page of the syllabus in a large folio lecture-notebook and annotate the page around the generous margins, adding definitions, references, underlining and stressing certain points and sometimes developing a point at some length. For example in an introductory note to one lecture early on in a series, geological method is defined in the following way:

> Like every other branch of natural science founded on observation, we observe that the great mixed masses of the earth's crust are arranged

I can only fire your imagination

in natural groups, and that the groups succeed in regular order. In describing each group we follow the methods of natural history, whether we describe the animal species or their organic content. In the arrangement of the groups we often desert that method and follow a chronological order of superposition. (Sedgwick, unpublished MS., n.d.)

The notes also bear out Professor Seeley's observations, that Sedgwick's aim was not to flood the audience with the minute trivia of 'facts', but to elucidate a clear and logical story. Lectures, for Sedgwick, were not intended to be a replacement for books, rather an introduction to books, opening up ideas and ways of thinking:

> His aim was essentially synthetic. He tried to establish habits of thinking about the larger phenomena of nature, and the interest he aroused was partly based on the principle of contrast and partly created by making the discoverers narrate their contribution to knowledge.
> (Clark and Hughes, 1890, vol. II: 489)

A unique record of one impressionable undergraduate's reaction to Sedgwick's lectures has been noted by Dr Colin Forbes, the present curator of the Sedgwick Museum, in the letters and notebook of one Richard Wilton, (1827–1903) an undergraduate student of Divinity at St Catharine's between 1847 and 1850. Wilton was totally captivated by the appearance and manner of Sedgwick, who was now in his sixties:

> Whilst gazing on his time-worn, weather-beaten face, you cannot help remembering that it is no idle spectator you are listening to, but a philosopher, indeed... I wish you could have heard the lecture in which he alluded to these travels and described 'the groaning among the Alps' caused by falling Avalanches. I sat rapt. He is indeed a grand living example of the truth of Wordsworth's philosophy. He has been schooled by Nature into a 'divine old man'.

Wilton, a minor poet, responded to the richness and vitality of Sedgwick's language and speculated on the degree to which Tennyson had been influenced by the old geologist:

> At twelve o'clock I go to the Geological Lecture. Coleridge used to attend Sir Humphrey Davy's lectures, he said, in order to increase his stock of metaphors: and anyone might, with advantage, attend Sedgwick's merely for the same purpose though he were uninterested by the mysterious truths he develops. His lectures are a rich mine of strong, rugged and picturesque English, and I am confident Tennyson has worked it assiduously. I could quote many passages to prove that he has studied and imitated Sedgwick's grand, nervous style. (Wilton, 1849b)

Nor is such speculation entirely without foundation. Alfred Tennyson was an undergraduate at Trinity between 1827 and 1831, and though he rejected most of the dons as 'none but dry-headed, calculating, angular little gentlemen' (Buckley, 1960: 22), he was a devoted student of Connop Thirlwall (1797–1875), the Broad Church radical and close associate of Sedgwick. Thirlwall fought long and hard, with the support of Sedgwick, for reform of the University, including the admission of Dissenters. He was an honorary member of the student Cambridge Conversazione Society, known as *The Apostles,* prominent members of which included Tennyson and the charismatic Arthur Hallam (1811–1833), the youth whose tragic death was the inspirational force behind Tennyson's great elegy *In Memoriam*, published in 1850. Given Tennyson's admiration of Thirlwall and his circle, his attendance at one or more of Sedgwick's lectures would have been a strong possibility. Undoubtedly, Sedgwick had a striking presence: 'almost six feet high, spare but strongly built, never bald, close-shaven, with dark eyes and complexion, strongly marked features, overhanging forehead, and bushy eyebrows' (Bonney, 1897).

Little wonder, therefore, that Sedgwick's lectures were so immensely popular both with students and with townspeople. Although only required to give four a year under the conditions of John Woodward's will, in 1820 he could inform the Vice Chancellor and Heads of College that he had given 22 public lectures and could request that this fact should entitle him to an increased stipend. This was, in fact, increased to £200 on condition that he gave 15 additional lectures each year, on top of the four he was required to do, and for the next half century Sedgwick's geological lectures were one of the features of Cambridge life, and were attended by large and enthusiastic audiences. His inspirational qualities, summed up by a statement made at one of his lectures, 'I cannot promise to teach you all geology, I can only fire your imaginations' (Clark and Hughes, 1890, vol. II: 490), must, if the many comments and accounts of his skill that have been recorded are to be accepted, make Sedgwick one of the greatest scientific lecturers and teachers of his day.

It was clear that he took great pleasure and even excitement in his lecturing. It was as if an audience, even during his extended periods of ill-health and lassitude, could force the adrenalin into his veins and, like an actor going on stage, he could almost invariably deliver a performance of often dazzling intellectual virtuosity and emotional vitality. That shrewd commentator Archibald Geikie has given a striking metaphorical insight of his own into the qualities that made a Sedgwick lecture. Commenting on a paper of Sedgwick's to the

Geological Society printed in the *Transactions of the Geological Society* he notes:

> Embalmed in the Society's printed publications, the paper, as we read it now, bears about as much resemblance to those who heard it, as the dried leaves do to the plant which tossed it, blossoms in the mountain wind. The words are there, but the fire and humour with which they rang through that dingy room in Somerset House has passed away.
> (Giekie, 1875, vol. I: 195)

At one anniversary dinner, Professor Ramsey was heard to remark that 'Sedgwick made the great speech of the evening. By turns he made us cry and roar with laughter, as he willed. His pathos and wit were equally admirable' (Woodward, 1907: 172). This gives an indication of how completely Sedgwick was able to control his audience.

Sedwick's lecturing activities were by no means confined to the University or meetings of the Geological Society. Throughout his professional life, he gave his time freely to numerous amateur scientific organizations, from the most prestigious to the most local, an involvement in what would now be termed adult education in the fullest sense of the word. This involvement went beyond merely giving a lecture or paper. It often involved the foundation or development of an organization.

Of these, none could have been more influential than the Cambridge Philosophical Society. It began during the tour made by Sedgwick and Henslow on the Isle of Wight, initially as an idea for a corresponding society, but finally, at a meeting in Cambridge in November 1819 a Society was founded for the purpose of 'promoting scientific enquiries and facilitating the communication of facts connected with the advancement of Philosophy and Natural History' (Hall, 1969: 11).

Sedgwick and Henslow were able successfully to overcome any possible hostility from the senior members of the University. As Rupert Hall, historian of the Society, has observed, when the Society was founded reaction among older dons varied from mirth, fears of its effect on discipline, to general indifference; a few even responded with favour.

The regular meetings were held, at which such topics as mathematics, various branches of scientific enquiry, architecture and economics were discussed. By 1820 there were 171 members and it quickly became an intellectual focal point for the brilliant younger generation of scholars, who were mainly Whig in politics, liberal in outlook, of Broad Church sympathy and were developed in that intellectual brotherhood of shared concern, described in later years

Letter from Sedgwick to Murchison seeking help for the Astronomer Royal and complaining of his health.

as 'The Cambridge Network' (Cannon, 1964). As well as Sedgwick (whose first geological paper was published by the Society) and Henslow, the Society attracted such men as Charles Babbage, the gifted mathematician, J. F. W. Herschel (1738–1822), the physicist and astronomer, George Peacock, the astronomer, George Airy (1801–1892), Astronomer Royal (1835–1881), David Brewster (1781–1868), the Scottish mathematician and philosopher, and that remarkable philosopher, scientist, mathematician and polymath, the energetic William Whewell. As Hall writes:

> 'The foundation of the Cambridge Philosophical Society in 1819 was the first positive step taken in modern times towards the emergence of Cambridge University as a great centre of teaching and research in

science. It was the move from almost a century of indolence and dullness during which, if Newton's name had been revered, his own example of relentless intellectual activity had rarely been followed. (Hall, 1969: 2)

Sedgwick's involvement in that other great reforming agency of science, the British Association for the Advancement of Science was less direct, but nonetheless profound.

David Brewster, like Charles Babbage, had published a diatribe about the failure of the universities, government and learned societies to halt the decline of science, this time in the *Quarterly Review,* and wished to establish, in Britain, an equivalent of the Deutscher Naturforsch Versammlung, a group of German scientists who met regularly in different cities in Germany. On February 23rd, 1831 Brewster wrote to John Phillips, who was then secretary of the Yorkshire Philosophical Society, to see if that society (which had been formed in 1822) would organize a British Association of Men of Science in York (Orange, 1973).

Many of the country's leading scientific men were invited to that first meeting, to be held at the end of September. In spite of scepticism from the academic establishment, among those to accept invitations were John Dalton and Murchison. Sedgwick received a formal invitation, on behalf of the Yorkshire Philosophical Society from Phillips and his Vice President Vernon Harcourt, who 'having received intimation from men of Scientific eminence in various parts of the Kingdom that a Meeting of the Friends of Science should be held in York during the last week in September next, we are directed to announce that the Society has offered the use of its apartments for the Accommodation of the Meeting...'. But scrawled on the invitation was a note in Phillips' handwriting:

My Dear Sir,
We hope you will have an excursion with us. If not pray send us a paper to enlighten the Edinburghians.
Yours truly, John Phillips

Naturally, this is a reference to David Brewster and his friends. Unfortunately Sedgwick had made arrangements to begin his work on the Cambrian rocks in North Wales and he wrote to Murchison from Wales:

I should be a traitor to quit my post now I am keeping a watch among the mountains. It would be delightful to mingle among the philosophers and commence deiphophist but it would be very bad philosophy in the long run. You may tell Mr Vernon that keeping away is a great act of self-denial on my part, and that I am in fact doing their work by staying away. (Clark and Hughes, 1890, vol. I: 380.)

Adam Sedgwick

The first meeting of the 'Philosophers and Provincials' was an enormous success, and it was decided to follow the German pattern (the Versammlung had now become the Gesellshaft Deutscher Naturforsch und Ärzte) and meet in different provincial centres, where it was hoped that the gathering would stimulate activity among local scientific communities. The objects of the Association were to: 'give a stronger impulse and more systematic direction to scientific enquiry, to obtain a greater degree of national attention to objects of science, and removal of those disadvantages which impede its progress, and to promote the cultivation of sciences with one another and with foreign philosophers' (Howarth, 1931).

The Association operated by dividing into a number of sections in various disciplines and in each section papers, which brought together the latest research, were presented by leading scientists. Each section had its own President, Vice President and Secretary. The annual meetings thus became, and remain to the present day, important scientific occasions when new ideas and areas of research were aired. They were also occasions of great conviviality, each centre striving to excel in its hospitality, and the after dinner speeches were famed for their eloquence.

The York philosophers tactfully chose Oxford and Cambridge for the next two meetings to ensure, successfully, the support of these two universities; Adam Sedgwick attended the Second Meeting, and from then took an important part in the Association's work, even though its meetings clashed with the one time of the year when prolonged field-work was a possibility. Nonetheless, he was active in the Geology Section, acting as its President or Vice President when the occasion served, presenting papers, arguing, defending his position and often delighting the Association as a whole with speeches of quite legendary eloquence.

For example, at the Third Meeting of the Association, at Cambridge, Sedgwick was:

> the animating spirit, delighting everybody by his geniality, or thrilling them by his unpremeditated eloquence.' And to such good effect that one Dr Chalmers who attended, moved by the 'power and beauty' of Sedgwick's farewell address, was reported afterwards as saying that he 'had never met with natural eloquence so great as that of Sedgwick.
> (Clark and Hughes, 1890, vol. I: 406–7)

But Sedgwick's involvement in such occasions was not merely confined to the distinguished gathering of academics. He often took the opportunity to organize an impromptu field-trip with local working men. At the Newcastle meeting of 1838, for example, Sedgwick found himself giving an oration to a huge gathering of miners and artisans on the beach at Tynemouth:

> Sedgwick wound up on Saturday with a burst of eloquence (something in the way of a sermon) of astonishing beauty and grandeur.
>
> But this, I am told, was nothing compared to an out-of-door speech, address or lecture, which he read on the sea-beach of Tynemouth to some 3,000 or 4,000 colliers and rabble (mixed with a sprinkling of their employers) which has produced a sensation such as is not likely to die away for years. I am told by ear and eye witnesses that it is impossible to conceive the sublimity of the scene, as he stood on the point a little raised, to which he rushed as if by a sudden impulse, and led them on from the scene around them to the wonders of the coal-country below them, thence to the economy of a coal-field, then to their relations to the coal-owners and capitalists, then to the great principles of morality and happiness, and last to their relation to God, and their own future prospects. (Clark and Hughes, 1890, vol I: 515–16)

The mixture of geology, ethics and religion is significant in that it reflects Sedgwick's constant concern to relate science to broader social and religious issues, and, for that matter, resolving his dual role as scientist and clergyman which came to preoccupy him in later years.

At the Manchester meeting, in 1842, Sedgwick's involvement with working men, was, if anything even more dramatic. Although no 'leveller' in the sense of having Chartist sympathies, nonetheless, Sedgwick did startle his august audience when he recalled walking about in the city slums and factories 'amidst the smoke of chimneys and roar of engines':

> In talking to the men whose brows were smeared with dirt, and whose hands were black with soot, I fell upon the marks of intellectual minds, and the proofs of high character, and I conversed with men who, in their own way, and in many ways bearing upon the purpose of life, were far my superiors. I would wish the members of the British Association to mingle themselves with these artisans, in these perhaps overlooked corners of our great cities; for as I talked to them, the feeling prevailing in my mind was that of the intellectual capacity manifest in the humbler orders of the population in Manchester. This is a great truth which I wish all the members of this Association to bear away among them, that while the institutions and customs of man set up a barrier, and draw a great and harsh line between man and man, the hand of the Almighty stamps His finest impress upon the soul of many a man who never rises beyond the ranks of comparative poverty and obscurity... (Sedgwick, 1842)

This was the period when Frederick Engels was collecting material from the same grimy streets in Manchester, which led to his *Condition of the Working Class in England,* published in 1845; whilst Sedgwick's oratory typically emphasized the dignity of the working man trapped behind the 'barriers' of social class, Engels, and later Marx, looked at the barriers themselves. Nonetheless it was, by any standards, a remarkable speech.

Sedgwick's position was perhaps closer to the Scottish stonemason turned geologist Hugh Miller, whose poetic and evocative *Old Red Sandstone* (1841) is rightly regarded as one of the classics of scientific literature. Miller advises 'young working men' not to attend Chartist meetings, but to read good books and learn to make 'a right use of the eyes' in scientific observation because: 'if all your minds are cultivated, not merely intellectually, but morally also, you would find yourselves, as a body, in the possession of a power which every charter in the world could not confer upon you and which all the tyranny of the world could not withstand' (Miller, 1841).

Sedgwick's field lectures were almost as famous as the public lectures; the students, up to 40 or 50 in number would gather on horseback and gallop to a chosen spot, where Sedgwick would dismount to describe a particular item or feature before continuing further afield, generally continuing until late into the afternoon when those with stamina and enthusiasm enough to stay with Sedgwick would return to Cambridge, often having covered up to 50 miles.

John Phillips records the sheer *joie de vivre* of a typical Sedgwick field trip, by boat up the River Cam to Ely:

> Never was a man so universally welcome among the members, and especially the junior members of his own university. Wonderful was the enjoyment of a voyage to Ely with a happy crew of his pupils (1850). If one stopped at Upware, the oolite there uplifted became the topic of an amusing and uplifted discourse; the great cathedral was visited in a more serious mood; the shores rang with the merriment of the returning boat; and the evening closed with a joyous banquet in the hospitable college rooms.   (Phillips, 1873)

However, in spite of the pressure of work on him, he was still able to give time to smaller societies at Cambridge, Ely and Norwich, where, not surprisingly he helped establish the local scientific Society not only giving a lecture 'distinguished by the eloquence and scientific research for which the learned Professor is celebrated' but by establishing a course of lectures.

The 1820s and 1830s were, of course, a period of 'Geological Mania' when countless small societies, of amateurs and devotees, were in operation, and the Mechanics Institutes, following Birkbeck's London Mechanics Institute, founded by George Birkbeck of Settle in 1823, were springing into being (Morell, 1971). Often, this amateur geology was of an extraordinary high quality, containing much original research. As David Allen has noted, in the first half of the nineteenth century there was: 'almost a total absence of a separate world of professional science'—a way in which the first half of the Victorian age differed quite sharply from the second' (Allen, 1976). Sedgwick was deeply involved in this great educational movement in amateur geology and natural history, both as an inspirational force as much as an educator.

Nowhere is this involvement with a small local society better illustrated than at Kendal where the Kendal Natural History and Scientific Society flourished in the 1830s and 1840s. The Society was founded in 1835 by a small group of keen local amateurs, including Thomas Gough, a local surgeon, Cornelius Nicholson, a local millowner and enthusiastic local historian, and Francis Danby, a curate. The Committee decided to seek the support and patronage of nearby men of science and letters, and accordingly wrote to George Birkbeck, William Wordsworth, John Dalton, Robert Southey and Adam Sedgwick to ask them to become Honorary Members. Most accepted.

But, on the realization that a more direct involvement would be useful, Gough and Nicholson were sent, in 1838, as a small deputation from Kendal to Dent to see if Professor Sedgwick would speak at their General Meeting. Sedgwick duly obliged and the Society received a 'very lucid and lengthened explanation of the great principles on which geology is founded' lasting around two hours and ending with an exhortation for 'Members to devote themselves to the study of Natural Sciences, and he was confident that the result would be an honour to the district and equal benefit to the cause of Science generally.' (Kendal Natural History and Scientific Society)

Not surprisingly, Sedgwick was elected President soon afterwards and remained President for 32 years as well as contributing generously to the foundation of their Museum. It is interesting to note that over 300 people came to Kendal to hear his Presidential address (considering the state of transport at the period this is an extraordinary testimony to local enthusiasm), which again lasted over two hours.

In 1844 he was urging ladies to get involved in scientific research and felt they had a particular contribution to make to agriculture and botany. At a period when the opportunities for higher education for women were virtually nil, a large percentage of Sedgwick's audiences were women and he often remarked about the 'blue-

Adam Sedgwick

stockings' of his audience, and duly encouraged them by his lectures.

The Kendal Minute Books are full of glowing tributes to the eloquence of Sedgwick's lectures and the harrassed reporter could only apologize that they were 'most animated and elegant, and that it is quite impossible to do justice to them in a limited abstract', praise that blended into an enormous affection as the years went by. It was a relationship of a great teacher—or actor—and his audience that is unimaginable to contemporary audiences. He could point out the 'glorious feast' opening out as the new railway lines—particularly Wordsworth's detested Kendal–Windermere railway—exposed the rock, 'laying bare the muscle' to allow the enthusiastic fossil-hunters to follow the navvies' picks.

It is interesting to note too, that the Society's programme of lectures, of which Sedgwick's was the jewel in the crown, cost 1s 6d ($7\frac{1}{2}$ pence) per head (no small sum in 1840s), with a reduction for a course of 4 lectures to 4s (20 pence). However, a member of a Mechanics Institute or working man recommended by a Subscriber was allowed in at the special reduced rate of 2s 6d ($12\frac{1}{2}$ pence) for the course. There was also a wide range of discussions and numerous topics in science, philosophy and the arts, in which members participated. But it was Sedgwick's lectures that were 'so numerously attended and listened too with such interest'.

It would be impossible to measure the true value of the involvement of this kind; large, enthusiastic audiences encouraged to undertake their own research, the widening impact of enthusiasm and interest spreading outwards like the circles of ripples from a stone dropped in a pond. One possible measure might be the amount of correspondence generated. There are, in the Cambridge University archives, boxes of letters from all over the world—from other scholars, professional geologists, mining engineers, surveyors, from South America, Russia, Canada, France, Germany, USA, India, wanting the technical advice, detailed information that Sedgwick could supply.

In a way this was to be expected. What is not expected, and therefore in its way is more exciting, is the correspondence, not from the specialists, but from the enthusiasts, the keen amateurs, giving details of things they have found or seen, asking for confirmation, or (very often) confirming a point that Professor Sedgwick had raised in a lecture. Almost invariably these people had been in the audience for one of Sedgwick's lectures—the Kendal letters are especially noticeable—and had gone away to continue their own work and research.

William Pearson, from Crossthwaite, for example, writes to recall

I can only fire your imagination

his observations on some boulders which suggest glaciation; J. Hudson, a collier from Bentham asks for the explanation of a detail; Thomas Sopwith indicates 'there will always be bed and board' when Sedgwick comes to Northumberland; or J. W. Farrer of Ingleborough Hall, grandfather of the great explorer and botanist Reginald Farrer, invites Sedgwick to explore the local cave system.

Perhaps the most exciting feature lay in the fact that men like Gough, Nicholson and Denby who had little formal geological background, were, as D. F. James relates: 'able to follow details of Sedgwick's work as he wrestled with the problems of palaeozoic stratigraphy at what were then the frontiers of knowledge. Today it is inconceivable that amateurs, however, enthusiastic, could participate usefully in geological research at this level, offering ideas and criticism to the Woodwardian Professor at Cambridge' (James, 1969).

The gap in the 1830s and 1840s between amateur and professional science was still a narrow one; the whole formalized, bureaucratic, technocratic specialization of science had not yet occurred. Thomas Gough, for example, could follow the intricate details of the Cambrian–Silurian controversy and, without any hint of deference, offer encouragement from the sidelines:

> The fossil evidence in your last paper is really thunderous and very severe critique upon that loose way of naming species by a mere birds eye view of a collection. To think that the May Hill fossils turn out to be either nearly all Wenlock species or new ones peculiar to the rock in which they occur, whereas one had got the notion hammered into one's head that they were all Caradoc. How will Sir Roderick and his friends get out of this mess?   (Gough, 1853)

The ultimate mark of a great teacher is the ability to alter minds, to bring about the birth of an intellect. It is a difficult accomplishment to measure, or to assess accurately. There was never a formal 'school' of Cambridge geologists in Sedgwick's time, but undoubtedly Sedgwick did succeed in developing that rare degree of intellectual excitement and feeling of spiritual awe in many of the pupils who were in contact with him.

This was amply demonstrated in the case of Joseph Beete Jukes (1811–1869) who came to Cambridge in 1833 with the serious intention of becoming a clergyman but when he 'sat in the geology classes week after week, enthralled by Sedgwick's lectures, all thought of a clerical career melted from Juke's mind' (Davies, 1969: 320). After graduating he wandered through the countryside with collecting bag and hammer, earning money by giving occasional lectures to the growing network of local societies.

At the request of Charles Darwin, Sedgwick and the 'Cambridge Network' helped get Jukes appointed as Geological Surveyor to Newfoundland in 1839–40; between 1842 and 1846 he went on an expedition to Australia and returned to join the staff of the Geological Survey at the salary of 9s (45 pence) per day, eventually becoming the Local Director of the Survey in Ireland and doing some extremely important work on fluvial theories (Davies, 1969).

Jukes, an almost fanatical disciple of Sedgwick's, and curiously one of the few 'pupils' (apart from Darwin) to achieve an international reputation, maintained a long and effusive correspondence with Sedgwick throughout a long and active professional life, much of it of considerable scientific interest in its own right.

If Adam Sedgwick was at the very least, 'a skillful instructor, a generous fellow-labourer and a bouyant companion' (Geikie, 1875: 139), was there any more to it than that? Clearly, he was a gifted lecturer, with a rare charisma, whether delivering a prepared paper or speaking extempore. He had the ability, too, to communicate to an audience, or to an individual, something of his total commitment and integrity, which was of more enduring value than any specific, factual information.

Jack Morrell (1977) has indicated how Sedgwick's committment to research was far from the accepted pattern of behaviour amongst mid-nineteenth century academic scientists, and how his Museum was used 'as a necessary part of both his teaching and research'. Jerry Ravetz has defined a quality he describes as a scientist's 'style'; such a subtle quality, difficult to define or isolate, may be the true key to the influence of a man like Sedgwick on English geology, both in the formal academic institutions and among the great amateur, naturalist tradition:

> Since the personal style of a matured scientist is influenced by his earlier experience, we can speak of a transmission of style from a master to his pupils. In this way one can construct intellectual genealogies; and to understand a man's work it may be relevant to know who was his teacher's teacher. This is clearly an important element in the creation of scientific 'schools'; and through the transmission of his personal 'style' of a great scientist even after he has departed and his own problems have become obsolete. But this interpersonal action is also conditioned by a style, that by which the scientist relates his personal scientific endeavour to the scientific communities of which he is a member. (Ravetz, 1971: 105–6)

But perhaps Martin Rudwick has provided the most complete assessment of Sedgwick's influence as a teacher:

I can only fire your imagination

Although Sedgwick's lectures were, until the latter part of his life, optional and extracurricular, they were immensely popular, and their influence on successive generations of Cambridge students, and hence on the shaping of English educated opinion on geology, is hard to overestimate (Rudwick, 1975).

9

Controversy II:
The Darwinian Revolution

Charles Darwin, whilst at Cambridge 'did not even attend Sedgwick's eloquent and interesting lectures' (De Beer, 1974: 33) largely owing to the fact that he had found Jameson's lectures, at Edinburgh University, so utterly boring that they had given him an aversion to geology. However, the young Darwin quickly came under the influence of Sedgwick's 'hiking companion' J. S. Henslow, by now Professor of Botany at the University.

Henslow persuaded Sedgwick to take Darwin with him on one of his summer field trips. So, in 1831 the young naturalist, now aged 22, accompanied Sedgwick on his important researches into the difficult Cambrian rocks of North Wales. Near Shrewsbury, an incident occurred which left an indelible impression on Darwin. In a gravel pit Darwin discovered a tropical shell fragment of the kind which was popular among local working people as chimney piece ornaments. Darwin's initial delight at the 'mysterious' find was quickly dampened by Sedgwick.

> But I was utterly astonished at Sedgwick not being delighted at so wonderful a fact as a tropical shell being found in the middle of England. Nothing before had made me thoroughly realise, though I had read various scientific books, that science consists of grasping facts so that general laws or conclusions could be drawn from them. (De Beer, 1974: 39)

The shell in fact, as Sedgwick indicated

> if really embedded there it would be the greatest misfortune to geology, as it would overthrow all that we know about the superficial deposits of the midland counties. These gravel beds belonged in fact to the glacial period, and in after years I found in them broken arctic shells. (De Beer, 1974: 39)

Controversy II: The Darwinian Revolution

Charles Darwin (1809–1882), aged 40.

The trip, from Darwin's point of view, in spite of Sedgwick's little eccentricities, proved a great success: 'Sedgwick often sent me on a line parallel to his, telling me to bring back specimens of the rocks and to mark the stratification on a map. I have little doubt that he did it for my good, as I was far too ignorant to have aided him' (De Beer, 1974: 39).

In Cwm Idwal Darwin was later to observe how the classic glacial phenomena—'a house burnt down by fire did not tell its story more plainly than did this valley. If it had been still filled by a glacier, the phenomena would have been less distinct than they are now' (De Beer, 1974: 40)—were totally unobserved by Sedgwick (or by Darwin himself at that time). This was, of course, several years before Louis Agassiz's (1807–1873) great work on Alpine glaciers and again served to indicate to Darwin how empirical observation is, to some extent, governed by scientific hypothesis.

Darwin's appointment to *The Beagle* was as W. F. Cannon (1964) suggests, very much a Cambridge 'Network' appointment; Sedgwick wrote to Darwin on the *Beagle* and contact between them was maintained largely through Henslow who, in a letter from Rio de Janeiro was asked to 'Tell Professor Sedgwick he does not know how much I am indebted to him for that Welsh expedition—it has given me an interest in geology which I would not give up for any consideration. I don't think I ever spent a more delightful three weeks than in the North Wales mountains'; or again from the Falkland Islands: 'tell him that I have never ceased being thankful for that short tour in Wales'.

Sedgwick helped Henslow in the identification of fossil and geological specimens sent back to Cambridge by Darwin. He had a high opinion of Darwin, who was delighted to hear that Sedgwick had 'said that [he] should take a place among the leading scientific men' (Barlow, 1974).

How did it come about, therefore, that when *Origin of Species* was published in 1859, Sedgwick was one of its leading opponents? To understand why, it is necessary to appreciate something of Sedgwick's own intellectual position.

The dominant philosophical view in Cambridge in the early part of the nineteenth century was derived from Archdeacon Paley's *Natural Theology* of 1802, which postulated a Universe established by a 'providential' Deity to a clearly understood design and with a benign purpose:

> There cannot be a design without a designer; contrivance without a contriver; order without choice; arrangement, without anything capable of arranging; subserviency and relation to a purpose without that which could intend a purpose; means suitable to an end without the end having been contemplated, or the means accommodated to it. Arrangement, disposition of parts, subserviency of means to an end, relation of instruments to an use imply the premise of an intelligence and mind.
> (Paley, 1802: 16)

Natural theology was the 'higher meaning' of natural philosophy, or science as it became more widely known, and scientific enquiry was the handmaid of true religion. Paley's famous image of the watch indicated the role of the scientific enquirer: 'when we come to inspect the watch, we perceive (what we could not discover in the stone) that it is put together for a purpose' (Paley, 1802: 16). Ultimately, it was an optimistic view: 'It is a happy world after all. The air, the earth, the water teem with delighted existence' (Paley, 1802: 28).

Although Sedgwick did not fully endorse all of Paley's theological utilitarianism, accepting more of a Kantian idealism, in his most extended statement of a personal philosophy, the *Discourse on the Study of the University* (which was originally the text of a commemorative sermon given at Trinity in 1832, published by popular request of students, and reissued at various times with the addition of massive Appendices and Prefaces), he gives a forceful statement of this position:

> Geology, like every other science when well intepreted, lends its aid to natural religion. It tells us, out of its own records, that man has been but a few years a dweller on the earth; for traces of himself and his works are confined to the last monuments of its history. Independently of every written testimony, we therefore believe that man with all his powers and appertencies, his marvellous structure and fitness for the world was called into being a few thousand years of the days in which we live. (Sedgwick, 1850: 26)

Life was created on the planet by an omnipotent and ever-present Intelligence who constantly interfered with his handiwork, perhaps through the medium of geological 'catastrophes' that cleared away one age of the earth's history and introduced new species or life forms marvellously adapted for their surroundings. Man, therefore, was placed on the earth by a 'personal Creator', who, once having established the Universe, remains as a 'pervading intelligent principle'. Geology itself

> tells us that God has not created the world and left it to itself, remaining ever after a quiescent spectator of his own work: for it puts before our eyes the certain proofs that during successive periods there have been, not only great changes in the external conditions of the earth, but corresponding changes in organic life—and that in every said instance of change, the new organs, so far as we can comprehend their use, were exactly suited to the functions of the beings they were given to. It shows intelligent power not only contriving means adapted to an end: but at many successive times contriving a change of mechanism adapted to a change of external conditions; and thus affords a proof, peculiarly its own, that the great first course contrives a provident and active intelligence. (Sedgwick, 1850: 27)

Yet Sedgwick had no patience for the 'Scriptural' or 'Mosaic' geologists who took a fundamentalist position and attempted to distort geological findings to fit with a naive and literal interpretation of the Bible. Sedgwick's position fitted the facts as he saw them, but he was willing to admit there could be difficulties:

> But let us for a moment, suppose that there are some religious difficulties in the conclusions of Geology. How are we then to solve them? Not by making a world after a pattern of our own—not by shifting and shuffling the solid strata of the earth, or dealing them out in such a way as to play the game of an ignorant and dishonest hypothesis—not by shutting our eyes to the facts, or denying the evidence of our senses: but by patient investigation carried on in the sincere love of truth and by learning to reject every consequence not warranted by direct physical evidence. (Sedgwick, 1850: 111)

For a clergyman, this was a courageous statement; truth could not be distorted to fit belief; truth had to be faced. He compared the more naive Scriptural geologists with a Brahmin who would deny the evidence of his senses: 'A Brahmin crushed with a stone the microscope that showed him living things among the vegetables of his daily food. The spirit of the Brahmin lies in Christendom' (Sedgwick, 1850: 112).

It was not at all surprising, therefore, when at the Second York Meeting of the British Association in 1844, when the Very Reverend William Cockburn (1773–1853), Dean of York, read a paper entitled 'Critical Remarks on certain passages in Dr Buckland's Bridgewater Treatise' to the Geological Section (later published under the astonishing title of *The Bible defended against the British Association*), which was a somewhat clumsy attack on geology from a naive, Mosaic viewpoint, that Adam Sedgwick, as one of the leading liberal scientists and Churchmen of the day, was asked to reply to it. This he did with a characteristic blend of wit and trenchant scholarship (Howarth, 1931: 59).

However just as Sedgwick attacked the more naive defender of the Bible, he was equally scathing, and for similar scientific reasons, of the holders of other theories and beliefs that were not supported by reasonable empirical evidence.

Of these theories, none caused him more anger than the theory of the 'transmutation of species'. Although it had an intellectually respectable history, from de Maillet and Erasmus Darwin (grandfather of Charles) in the eighteenth century, and the great Lamarck at the turn of the nineteenth century, Sedgwick regarded it as hopelessly unscientific because it was a hypothesis that was based on too little evidence and seemed to contradict the clear evidence of Cuvier, Elie de Beaumont and others.

In 1844, however, an anonymous work *The Vestiges of the Natural History of Creation* was published. Although its authorship was for

Controversy II: The Darwinian Revolution

long a secret, it was written by Robert Chambers (1802–1871), the Edinburgh publisher and popularizer of science, famous with his brother for the *Penny Journal,* a popular scientific journal of its day. Written in an 'agreeable style' by a non scientist (inevitably one of its critics suggested that the author 'knew no more science than might have been picked up from reading Chambers' Journal') it was in its way a considerable achievement, developing at some length the theory of a 'law of natural development' suggesting how life had evolved on earth from simpler to more complex creation, by a process of gradual transmutation.

Sedgwick, who had described 'transmutation of the species' (as early as 1834 in the *Discourse*) as 'a theory no better than a phrenzied dream', was quick to see many of the errors and absurdities of Chambers' work. But what really enraged him was that it so quickly became an extraordinary success, going through several editions (with some of the worst errors tastefully revised) and was widely read and highly influential.

The reasons for its success were not, it must be understood, purely scientific. *The Vestiges* touched a necessary chord of darkness, of pessimism and even despair in the Victorian imagination, the image of an empty, cruel Universe that mocked conventional faith, far removed from the complacent optimism of Paley.

Tennyson's famous lines from *In Memoriam* indicated how geology had undermined old certainties of a benign 'nature':

> So careful of the type? but no.
> From scarped cliff and quarried stone
> She cries, 'A thousand types are gone:
> I care for nothing, all shall go.'

And it was difficult to maintain a Christian Faith when a young man read how 'Nature, red in tooth and claw, With ravine, shriek'd against his creed' (Tennyson, 1850).

The success of *The Vestiges* lay in the fact that it reflected this mood of doubt and uncertainty, yet a need, too, for a dynamic, changing universe, darkly hostile yet capable of growth and change, something raw, exciting, barbaric and essentially romantic:

> This world was once a fluid haze of light,
> Till towards the centre set the starry tides,
> And eddied its suns, that wheeling cast
> The planets: then the monster, then the man
> Tattoo'd or woaded, winter-clad in skins,
> Raw from the prime, and crushing down his mate;   (Tennyson, 1847)

Adam Sedgwick

Sedgwick was aware of the enormous influence of *The Vestiges* when he described it as 'a rank pill of asafoetida and arsenic covered with gold leaf', and in a letter to Lyell exploded into a diatribe:

> The sober facts of geology shuffled, so as to play a rogue's game; phrenology (that sinkhole of human folly and prating coxcombry); spontaneous generation; transmutation of species; and I know not what, all to be swallowed without tasting or trying like so much horse-physic'.
> (Clark and Hughes, 1890, vol II: 83–87)

From that time on his lectures and writings frequently contained an indignant attack on *The Vestiges,* which he believed, with uncharacteristic chauvinism, must have been written by a woman. When, *The Discourse,* was reprinted for the fifth time in 1850, it included a phenomenal 442 page 'Preface', which he confessed to R. B. Jukes included 'Geology, Psychology, Theology, Deism, Atheism, Pantheism, Procreation, Transmutation, Prothengenesis, Popery and Tom foolery—a long sermon or queer tract'. But the motivating force behind this colossal and unwieldly piece was a critique of the dreadful *Vestiges*. It was as if he believed he could somehow suppress Chambers by sheer weight and force of intellectual argument.

Darwin, reading a similar outburst from Sedgwick against *The Vestiges* in *The Edinburgh Review* in 1845, whilst working on his own version of the mutability of species, had to admit to Lyell that: 'It is a grand piece of argument against mutability of species and I read it with fear and trembling' (F. Darwin, 1887). It was predictable, therefore, that when the *Origin of Species* was finally published in 1859, Sedgwick would see it as another *Vestiges,* but more expert and, therefore, more dangerous. Rather courageously, Darwin sent him a copy of the first edition, also warning him that:

> As the conclusion at which I have arrived after an amount of work which is not apparent in this condensed sketch, is so diametrically opposed to that which you have often advocated with so much force, you might think I send my volume to you out of a spirit of bravado and with a want of respect, but I assure you I am activated by quite opposite feelings. (Clark and Hughes, 1890, vol. II: 356)

Sedgwick replied at length confessing he had:

> read your book with more pain than pleasure. Parts of it I admired greatly, parts I laughed at till my sides were almost sore; other parts I read with absolute sorrow, because I think them utterly false and mischievous. You have *deserted* after a start in that tram-road of all solid physical truth—the true method of induction, and started off in machinery as wild, I think, as Bishop Wilkie's locomotive that was to sail with us to the moon. (Clark and Hughes, 1890, vol II: 356-7)

He continued to outline parts of the book that offended his 'moral taste' including the 'tone of triumphant confidence in which you appeal to the rising generation'.

Darwin's reply reflected his sense of deep hurt at Sedgwick's 'severe disapprobation and ridicule', and was able, perhaps unknowingly, to refer back to Sedgwick's own confident assertions about the ultimate victory of scientific truth: 'I do not think my book will be mischievous; for there are so many works that, if I be wrong, I shall soon be annihilated; and surely you will agree that truth can be known only by rising victorious from every attack' (Clark and Hughes, 1890, vol. II: 359).

The story of the success of the *Origin of Species* is too well known to require repetition here; Darwin had many powerful advocates of the calibre of Thomas Huxley and Herbert Spencer (1820–1903), assisted by Bishop Wilberforce's foolish performance, which rallied opinion to Darwin. The Darwinians were soon attracting most radical young scientists to their cause.

Sedgwick was, in fact, because of his honesty, integrity and fine scientific mind perhaps the most serious antagonist of the *Origin*. His long anonymous letter in *The Spectator* in March 1860 restated his position that Creation was a divine act:

> Change the conditions and old species would disappear, and new species *might* be seen to come and flourish. But how, and by what cause? I say by *creation*. But, what do I mean by creation? I reply, the operation of a power quite beyond the powers of a pigeon-fancier, cross-breeder or hybridiser; a power I cannot imitate or comprehend—but in which I believe, by a legitimate conclusion of sound reason draws from the laws of harmonies of nature. For I can see all around me a design and purpose, and a mutual adaptation of parts which I can comprehend and which proves that there is exterior to and above the mere phenomenon of Nature a great prescient and designing aim. Believing this, I have no difficulty in understanding the appearance of new species during successive epochs of the earth.

It is too simplistic, with the advantage of hindsight, to dismiss Sedgwick as being 'wrong'. Many capable scientists objected to the Darwinian hypothesis for well-argued valid reasons based on good scientific principles; they could easily have been right, and it is too easy with what Mandelbaum calls the 'retrospective fallacy' to see the development of nineteenth century scientific progress purely in terms of Darwin and the Darwinians.

Clearly, by 1859, Sedgwick, now in his mid-70s, was not capable of reading the *Origin* with any degree of open mindedness. He was not a biologist by training, and whilst, at least in the Cambridge Philisophical Society paper of 1860, confining his attack to the geological aspects of the theory, he was not in a position to assess fully the wealth of careful empirical detail brought by Darwin to his theory, which makes it so very much more than an elaboration of Chambers' tenuous hypothesis.

But Sedgwick's hostility to Darwinianism was far more than the reaction of a gouty, by now conservative, Academic and Churchman.

It is now seen, with some justification, that Darwin's work was merely the culmination of a whole cultural and scientific phenomenon, the cult of 'transformism' and 'evolution'. Darwin's role was as a kind of catalyst. He was the one truly great scientific figure who was capable, with infinite patience and empirical understanding, of putting together a fine scientific hypothesis from some of the more outrageous and less credible claims that had been made, and presenting the evidence to the scientific world in cool, rational prose. The result was a work which totally changed man's view of the Universe, moving him from a position in the centre of the stage, in a close relationship with God who had created him in his own image, to a defenceless, isolated figure on the fringe of creation who had merely survived a bleak struggle in a hostile environment, and who, in Spencer's words had succeeded to join 'the survival of the fittest'.

The prospect was frightening. As one Victorian scholar expressed it:

> Never in the history of man has so terrific a calamity befallen the race as that which all who look may now behold advancing as a deluge, black with destruction, resistless in might, uprooting most cherished hopes, engulfing our most precious creed, and bringing our highest life to a mindless desolation... The floodgates of infidelity are open, and Atheism overlooking is upon us.   (Romanes, 1878)

As Maurice Mandelbaum (1971: 77) points out, the debate about the relationship between religion and various branches of science had preoccupied leading scientists and theologians throughout the nineteenth century; therefore 'it was not the least surprising that the theological implications of Darwin's theory received the immediate and widespread attention that they did'.

Until the publication of the *Origin* it was perfectly possible for an empirical scientist to reconcile the teachings of the Old Testament with the discoveries of geology. Genesis, of course, was not to be taken literally and the Flood was only one of many catastrophes, such as had been so brilliantly demonstrated by Agassiz as having occurred not so very long ago even in the British Isles and which had changed the pattern of life on the planet. Even the Uniformitarian–Catastrophism debate was now reconciled by perceiving a broader time-scale for Catastrophes—which could still be understood as secular 'miracles', and by pursuing the line of argument so brilliantly presented by Sedgwick in his 1831 Presidential Address. This had included a searching critique of the first volume of Lyell's *Principles of Geology* and postulated a series of supernaturally created adaptations to changing eras.

The *Origin* had altered the whole metaphysical scenario, the shaping hand of God was removed to be replaced by a blind cruel law of power and adaptability, 'a dish of rank materialism', which many were quick to apply, with or without reason, to many other scientific disciplines or areas of human activity, including society itself. Here 'Social Darwinism' became a peculiarly unpleasant and inhumane creed, eventually justifying the most unpleasant excesses of capitalism, Marxism and National Socialism.

Sedgwick's unflinching opposition to the 'mutability of species' was not, therefore, as naive as is often imagined. It stemmed from a deep and humane commitment to certain fundamental human and moral truths, perhaps close to what would now be described as the 'social responsibility' of the scientist. His attacks on the 'degrading materialism' of Chambers and Darwin came, therefore, from a man who was well aware of their possible implications and manifestations.

Gillespie (1951: 150) has surely missed the point when he suggests that Sedgwick's outbursts were 'a cry from the heart of a scientist upon whom had suddenly flashed the full implications of his own endeavours and who refused to understand them. The very framework of society seemed threatened'. Sedgwick clearly understood the implications only too well, and, albeit wrong-headedly, wanted to use the techniques available to him—reason and rational argument—to prove things otherwise. His attempt to suggest that Darwin had left the 'tram-road of inductive reason' was an attempt to turn back the tide, even against his own scientific instinct.

The central point was the uniqueness of Man. The 'harmony and order,' which can be seen in the material world, infers the 'existence of an intelligent power superior to the dead matter which surrounds us', which we comprehend as the 'Godhead'. 'For man, by the exercise of his own forethought and will, can produce a series of orderly phenomena—feebly resembling the works of God, however inferior to them in vastness, in complexity, and in the sure indications of power and wisdom'. God's design, therefore, could be seen in the evolution of higher forms on the planet, 'the historical development of the forms and functions of organic life during successive epochs, which seems to mark a gradual evolution of Creative Power manifest by a gradual ascent towards a higher type of being'. This was not merely the result of 'material cause and material effect': 'They may maintain that what we call law is mere material order, and nothing else; that what we call adaptation is but a dream or fancy; that what we call intellect and mind is but a form of material manifestation; that conscience is but a material weakness; and that hopes of future good are but an idle material dream' (Sedgwick, 1850).

Sedgwick has here accurately diagnosed one of the causes of what the philosopher Philip H. Phenix describes as the 'meaninglessness' of contemporary society, a situation created by the dissolution of old certainties with little that is positive to replace them (Phenix, 1964). Far from being of merely historic interest, this is a debate which still has a considerable contemporary relevance and is far from resolution.

This problem could, and still does, worry the atheist as much as the Christian, and Thomas Huxley in his Romanes Lecture of 1893 *Evolution and Ethics,* postulated an 'ethical process' as a mechanism to prevent the overthrow of civilized values in a Universe that no longer contained a benign Creator:

> Men in society are undoubtedly subject to the cosmic process... The struggle for existence tends to eliminate those less fitted to adapt themselves to the conditions of their existence. The strongest, the most self-assertive tend to trample down the weaker... Social progress means a checking of the cosmic process at every step, and the substitution for it of another, which may be called the ethical process; the end of which is not the survival of those who may happen to be the fittest in respect of the whole of the condition which many obtain, but of those who are ethically the best. (Huxley, 1893)

As a Minister of the Church and a committed Christian, Sedgwick could not have accepted such a view. It denies the existence of a First Cause—the Almighty—and does not see the Universe in teleological terms, i.e. as having a purpose, except for the purpose that man himself, for ethical reasons, imposes on it. God has no place in Huxley's universe.

Had he been a younger man, and not a committed Christian in the sense of being a Minister of the Church, Sedgwick might have been able to move towards a Huxleyite position. After all, it did see the Universe in something like humanistic teleological terms, with

Controversy II: The Darwinian Revolution

higher forms (i.e. ethically sound) eventually emerging. But the First Cause—the Godhead—was replaced by man himself, now controlling his own destiny at the pinnacle of Creation.

David Hull has given an admirable summary of how Darwin inadvertently terminated the long, and close, relationship of science and theology, and how Sedgwick's abhorrence of his theory—however wrong-headed it may seem to us more than a century later—contained an element of truth:

> Not only were scientists making great contributions to the noble edifice of science and to mankind by application of science to medicine and industry, but their discoveries also lent support to religion through natural theology. As they showed more clearly how nature worked, they showed how great the creator's wisdom had been. In his youth Darwin had hoped to join in this great parade of scientists and men of God marching arm in arm to produce a better world. Instead he stopped it dead in its tracks. (Hull, 1974: 5–6)

> Sedgwick may not have been the greatest of philosophers, but he accurately diagnosed the danger which evolutionary theory posed for natural theology. Since Sedgwick was one of the most prominent advocates of natural theology in Victorian England, the danger was very real to him. Evolutionary theory was a dish of rank materialism, and it *did* repudiate the kind of reasoning from final causes that had been used to support belief in God. Sedgwick refused to eliminate completely God's direct involvement in natural phenomena. A universe governed completely by laws—even divinely instituted law—was devoid of significance for theology. (Hull, 1974: 15)

Many scientists of the day resolved this difficulty by simply compartmentalizing their scientific work away from their religious or ethical views. Sedgwick's fundamental honesty caused him to try and constantly reconcile the two, even when it meant praising a relatively poor scientific work, which had its theology right. In this respect he was essentially an eighteenth-century humanist and rationalist clinging to a world view which, though already archaic by 1860, we might have cause to envy.

10

The Prince and the Radical

Prince Albert's involvement with Cambridge University probably owed more to William Whewell, Master of Trinity, and Adam Sedgwick, by 1845 Vice-Master of Trinity, than to any two other individuals.

On the death of the Chancellor, the Duke of Northumberland in February 1847, Sedgwick persuaded a group of Fellows to support the invitation of Prince Albert to fill the vacant office. The suggestion received the support of Whewell who felt that a member of the Royal Family, being above the eternal squabbles between Whig and Tory that ran through University affairs, would prove a beneficial influence on University life. Moreover Albert was an intellectual, with wide interest in the arts and sciences, and clearly could offer a refreshing breadth of vision to University affairs.

The Queen and her advisors considered the question carefully; it was felt that Chancellor of the University of Cambridge was an appointment of suitable dignity and significance for the Prince Consort, and on the understanding that there would be no opposition, Albert allowed his name to be put forward. All seemed to be going well.

Unfortunately, a group of Tories in St John's thought differently. They decided to nominate a candidate of their own choice, who turned out to be the aged Lord Powis, described by Adam Sedgwick, doubtless with a degree of accuracy as 'a deaf old woman' (Winstanley, 1840: 108).

To the consternation of liberal opinion at Cambridge, Prince Albert, fearful of the consequence of someone as close as he was to the Sovereign herself being involved in an election, withdrew. Whewell, infuriated, tried to use his considerable influence to get Powis to withdraw, but without success. Appeals were made to the

Prince Albert, Consort of Queen Victoria (1819–1861)

Prince. Albert by now was eager to involve himself in University affairs, realizing that he could use his influence to bring about desperately needed reforms: 'Academically, Cambridge had not yet emerged from the eighteenth century. During most of the first half of the nineteenth century, its scholarship was derided on the Continent, as Albert would have known' (Pound, 1973: 189). So a subtle compromise was struck. Albert would agree to be nominated 'without his consent'. The progressives felt that there would be little risk of defeat, and success seemed assured.

However, a strong current of opposition ran against the Prince. If he was Chancellor this would be a threat to the traditional independence of the University; could not the Sovereign, through her Consort, have power to interfere in its affairs? Worse, Albert was a German—a wave of xenophobia ran through the University. Should an ancient University have a young foreigner, a *German*, notwithstanding his alleged intellectual brilliance or his relationship with the Queen, as Chancellor?

Sedgwick, moving away from any pretension of neutrality, urged as much support as he could for the Prince. But the election seemed very much in the balance. When the ballot was counted the results were unnervingly close. Albert received 617 votes, the hapless Lord Powis 602. Though he had won the election, the narrowness of the margin, and against such a feeble rival candidate, revealed a strong anti-royal feeling. Albert, distressed, wavered. Should he accept?

The shrewd Sir Robert Peel, realizing the considerable advantage that there would be in having a man of Albert's energy and imagination in the Chancellorship, encouraged him to accept. Accordingly, when an official invitation came from the University asking him to accept the post of Chancellor, he did so, and on July 5th, 1847 was installed amidst enormous enthusiasm and splendour, much to the obvious relief of Queen Victoria who informed Sedgwick that 'she was delighted with her reception, and wished to express herself in the strongest terms' (Pound, 1973: 191).

Sedgwick's association with the Royal Family had recently been made closer when, soon after the Prince's election, in April 1847, he was appointed as the Chancellor's secretary. Winstanley (1940) has argued that Sedgwick's appointment as Prince Albert's secretary 'has no significance' and it was merely the kind of recognition which a scholar of Sedgwick's eminence and seniority might receive in the form of an honorary appointment. This is surely a naive view. Sedgwick was already well known—notorious might be the view—for his outspoken attacks against the Cambridge Establishment, which age had certainly not softened. Politically he was well to the left of this Establishment, showing his father's almost envangelical detestation of slavery and other infringements of human rights.

Naturally enough he was a vocal supporter of the Reform Bill at a time when most of the University was totally opposed to it (Clark and Hughes, 1890, vol. I: 373–4).

It was Sedgwick, for example, in 1834 who had to lead the unsuccessful campaign to abolish religious 'tests', which involved petitioning both Houses of Parliament and writing a forceful letter to The Times. These 'tests' forced all members of the University writing to take degrees to, at least nominally, be Anglican, and kept Dissenters and Catholics out of Universities. It was affirmed by the conservatives that tests were essential for 'sound religious instruction and discipline' Sedgwick's response to Bishop Blomfield, who sent him a copy of his own speech in the Lord's attacking the 62 petitioners, is a masterly piece of controlled polemic:

> As a great learned and scientific University giving degrees in all the learned faculties—incorporating as a lay body, and only regarded as such in the eyes of the law of England—Cambridge may stand firmly... But if she once be considered as a mere school for the Church Establishment her endowments will be thought out of all reasonable dimensions, and before many years are over we may see our noble edifices beginning to crumble about our ears. (Clark and Hughes, 1890, vol.I: 424-5).

Again, when Tennyson's gifted tutor, Connop Thirlwall, denounced the system of compulsory attendance at chapel, in a pamphlet, it was Sedgwick who was asked to be the spokesman for the liberal faction and who led a deputation to see the despotic Dr Wordsworth, Master of Trinity, who had forced Thirlwall to resign (Clark and Hughes, 1890, vol. I: 425-6).

As a natural democrat, with the traditions of the Dentdale Statesmen behind him, Sedgwick was frequently the leader of various campaigns to loosen the tyrannical hold of the College 'Heads' or Principals, whose statutes went back to the time of Elizabeth I, by means of deputations, petitions, meetings and letters, including letters in the local newspapers. Equally the power of the Vice Chancellor, a position of great prestige and autocracy in the University was something that Sedgwick and his colleagues—men like Whewell, Peacock, Airey and others—resented. The Senate, though partially elected, was itself subject to the vote of a body known as the Caput, which could prevent matters being referred to the Senate.

This degree of involvement in the liberal cause did not bring automatic popularity. If you did not share Sedgwick's particular view point, his passionate outbursts might seem to reflect a personality which was 'extremely violent, dogmatic and unfair, giving vent to an indignation which he pleased to think righteous', or even worse 'aggressive, dogmatic and too ready to think of himself as battling against the forces of darkness and evil (Winstanley, 1940).

Such a reputation would not be unknown to as shrewd a political adviser as Sir Robert Peel, who, if not too concerned about the 'forces of darkness and evil' was concerned about the stagnant self-interest and complacent conservatism of the ancient universities.

Equally telling perhaps, was Sedgwick's remarkable intellectual breadth. The *Discourse on the Studies of the University* has a sound grasp, not only of scientific, mathematical and religious disciplines, but also a refreshingly modern conception of a humane, liberal education and of a balanced educational curriculum, in which the ethical, imaginative, aesthetic and linguistic are part of a whole which includes the rational and the scientific. Take for example his statement on the purposes of literature. Sedgwick was himself an enthusiastic reader of Defoe, Swift, Shakespeare, Scott, Wordsworth—which, with little alteration, could have been taken for the pages of Matthew Arnold, John Ruskin, John Dewery, Herbert Read, or any contemporary apologist of the value of literature in education:

> But surely it is our glorious privilege to follow the track of those who have adorned the history of mankind—to feel as they have felt—to think as they have thought—and to draw from the living fountain of their genius. Close and animating is the intellectual communion we hold with them! Visions of imagination starting from their souls, as if struck out by creative power, are turned into words, and fixed in the glowing forms of language: and, by a law of our being not under our control, kindle within us the very fire which (it may be thousands of years ago) warmed the bosom of the orator in part—so that once again, for a moment, he seems in word and feeling, to have a living presence within our selves!
> (Sedgwick, 1834: 34)

Such a breadth of vision, perhaps unfortunately, would not be readily associated with a modern specialist teacher of academic geology. The *Discourse*, which began life as a Commemorative Sermon, was printed and reprinted four times by popular request with the elephantine Preface, Appendices and Supplements making it a unique and peculiarly Sedgwickian form of treatise, and doubtless established Sedgwick's reputation as an educationalist with the breadth of vision necessary to see where new curricular developments should come.

Neither should we imagine that the lack of letters between Sedgwick and Prince Albert suggests that his influence was minimal. The key decisions and exchanges of ideas took place in informal meetings, in Cambridge, at Windsor, at Osborne. The Prince's task was formidable. Peel had warned him: 'You will be struck with the *total* absence of study of History and of those of all modern *real* sciences, as well as metaphysical' (Pound 1973: 171). Whilst Albert drew Peel's attention to the neglect of political economy and law studies.

The Cambridge Academic Establishment was soon to discover that Albert was more than a mere regal figurehead, when the Prince sent for University examination papers and returned them to the university suitably inscribed with critical comments. This must have been something of a shock, but it was a mere squib compared with what was to follow.

The Prince and the Radical

In December of 1847 the Queen invited Sedgwick to Balmoral. Her secretary, Colonel Phipps wrote with the usual delicacy; 'The Prince thinks a little change of air will do you good'.

Sedgwick spent three days in the royal household. He has left a delightful account of the visit in a letter to his niece, Isabella. At the time of the visit Osborne was still undergoing alterations and on arrival Sedgwick was delighted to note 'Carts, toys and other signs of young children, scattered about the hall in considerable confusion. Human nature is the same whatever rank, and with whatever garb it may be covered'; and amongst the details he records about the Queen was her evident shyness in company—she blushed when rising to speak to him for the first time. He also observed the intriguing fact that she and Albert would sing together 'before the ladies in waiting; but the Queen does not like to sing before the gentlemen'. Whilst at Osborne, he also acted as the family chaplain.

What really struck Sedgwick on this visit was the intellectual breadth and cultivated charm of Albert:

> He is a well-read man, whose mind is admirably cultivated in many departments little studied by our young noblemen, and he is often undervalued by stupid persons who have no true conception of his real character, and no power of estimating his sound and very extensive knowledge. He is called proud and formal. I have not found him so; but on the contrary, kind, frank and courteous.

However, this was no courtesy invitation to Osborne. In Albert's study the real purpose of the visit became clear: 'His Royal Highness then entered at great length on the studies of the University and has, I am certain, the deepest interest in the well being of Cambridge.... Our discussion lasted nearly two hours' (Clark and Hughes, 1890, vol.II: 131–40).

The influence of Prince Albert was seen as early as 1848, when two new Triposes were established, in Moral Sciences and Natural Sciences, together with a scheme to ensure that every degree candidate attended at least one course of professorial lectures. As a delighted *Times* leader writer expressed it; 'The change in the curriculum of Cambridge Education, which was announced yesterday, has taken everybody by surprise. We knew the event must come, but we did not look for its attainment without an arduous struggle' (*The Times*, October 31st, 1848).

Adam Sedgwick was responsible for the geological papers in the Natural Science Tripos between 1851 and 1860. Roy Porter has written of the significance of this development in establishing the 'competitive excellence', which was to transform Cambridge into one of the leading centres of scientific research in Western Europe.

In a detailed examination of Sedgwick's examination papers in geology in the Cambridge University archives, Dr Porter has suggested that Sedgwick's papers 'possessed a breadth, freshness and intellectual vigour unparalleled elsewhere' which reflected Sedgwick's own conception of geological education in the broadest sense:

> The emphasis was on thought, not facts. The questions were broad, interpretative, untechnical. There was little on the chemistry of mineral composition or the exact location of fossils. Some of Sedgwick's papers possessed an imaginative grasp of educational purpose which makes equivalent papers elsewhere—and after in Cambridge—appear dull and routine.   (Porter, 1977b).

An examination has an inevitable feed-back into the teaching system; this breadth of vision would have forced itself upon undergraduates and been an extraordinary stimulus to geology in Cambridge during that decade.

More obvious reforms were also afoot. Lord John Russell, the new Prime Minister and a shrewd politician, in 1847, had informed Prince Albert that he was in favour of advising the Queen to 'appoint a Commission to inquire into the state of Schools and Colleges of Royal Foundation' and further support came early in 1848 from a document, signed by 224 graduates of the Universities, calling for a Royal Commission of Inquiry 'into the best methods of securing the improvement of the Universities of Oxford and Cambridge' (Clark and Hughes, 1890, vol. II: 170–1).

Meanwhile, a syndicate had been formed to examine the stature of the University and to suggest internal reforms including the broadening of the curriculum, but this did not reduce the external pressure for change. It was clearly Albert's hope that the reforms could be achieved from within the University. As he wrote to Sir Robert Peel:

> [Sir Robert] will have been pleased by results at Cambridge by which the foundation for a better University education has been laid and the Universities may be saved from attacks upon their constitutions which were being prepared. The University will have been astonished in the public press upon these improvements and the faults of the old system.
> (Pound, 1973)

However, James Heywood, a Member of Parliament for a Lancashire constituency and one of the architects of the 1848 petition, pressed a motion through the House of Commons that Russell found himself having to accept, 'praying that Her Majesty would be graciously pleased to issue her Royal Commission of Inquiry into the state of the Universities and Colleges at Oxford, Cambridge and Dublin' (Clark and Hughes, 1890, vol. II: 171).

This not only took Albert by surprise, but sent shocks of alarm and gloom through the leafy quadrangles of Cambridge, and soon a powerful rearguard action was being organized led by Heads of Houses, Professors and Lecturers. But the wishes of Parliament would not be deterred by any illustrious Address, signed by 156 dons, to request the Vice Chancellor to seek Prince Albert's aid in protecting the ancient 'freedom, rights, statutes, possessions and useages' that now lay under a Parliamentary scrutiny.

Adam Sedgwick, as Vice Master of Trinity a senior member of the University, as well as being the Chancellor's Secretary, was in a difficult position. He wanted the reforms, but clearly had loyalty to his College, his colleagues, and the Prince, who was in favour of seeing internal changes. For this reason he refused to sign the 1848 petition. In May 1850, Lord John Russell wrote to Sedgwick to ask him to join the Bishop of Chester and the Dean of Ely to 'take part in the Labours of the Commission'. Sedgwick's loyalties were now deeply divided. He wrote to Prince Albert's Secretary and amanuensis, Colonel Gray, stating at some length his reasons for feeling he was unable to accept membership.

Colonel Gray's reply indicated how much Prince Albert would 'personally regret' Sedgwick's refusal to serve on the Commission arguing that it was 'most essential that the Commission should be formed of friends of the University'; and, in a later letter: 'HRH thinks that these objections are not such as should prevent your acceptance, he believes that your nomination as one of the Commissioners would have the best possible effect and your services on the Commission would be most valuable' (Clark and Hughes, 1890, vol. II: 180–1). Sedgwick could hardly refuse to accept after such a plea. Prince Albert had got his way. If he was forced to have a Royal Commission, he would make sure his men were on it.

With Sedgwick on the Commission were the Bishop of Chester, his old colleague George Peacock, now Dean of Ely, J. F. W. Herschel and Sir John Romilly. They appointed John Bateson of St John's as their secretary.

During 1851 and 1852 the Commission took up a great deal of Sedgwick's limited time, involving him in frequent meetings and a good deal of writing, visits to London, and another stay at Osborne in July 1852. Here Sedgwick found himself reading the family prayers, explaining the structure of some freak hailstone to the Queen (she and Albert having been caught in a 'terrific thunderstorm' on the preceding day near Ryde) and walking in the park with time to play ball with Prince Arthur ('a very fine merry child'; Clark and Hughes, 1890, vol. II: 221–226).

The purpose of the visit was, of course, to discuss in depth the forthcoming Report. It is clear that the close, personal relationship between Prince Albert and Adam Sedgwick, and the obvious empathy between them in spite of their contrasting backgrounds, had a profound impact on the Report, much of which was in fact written by Sedgwick himself. If nothing else it would ensure that the recommendations were in sympathy with the Prince's own liberal views. One might go further and see it as a radical alliance between two men of progressive views who were able to use their influence through the normal machinery of Government, to transform the University and, with it, the direction of Higher Education in England.

When the document was finally delivered by Sedgwick and John Bateson to the Queen's Printing Office, in August 1852, Sedgwick felt a great sense of relief. 'We felt as happy as does a mail-coach horse in reaching a stable after a hard drive' (Clark and Hughes, 1890, vol. II: 226).

It was a magnificent effort, both the Evidence and the actual Report, and the recommendations were such as to thrill the most progressive heart. The 'Caput' was to be abolished in favour of a democratic council; certain archaic privileges 'offensive to the town' were to be abolished; Boards of Studies for each department or learning were to be established; examinations were to be reformed; Fellowships and Scholarships were to be 'merit only', 'closed' scholarships were to be available to 'all of Her Majesty's subjects wherever born'; colleges would contribute towards the salaries of Lecturers and Professors; and, a typically Albert touch, new Museums of Science were to be erected.

Not surprisingly the Commission's Report was bitterly resented by the Heads of Colleges. In spite of the strength and authority of the recommendations, no action was taken on them from within the University. Vested interests were not unnaturally loathe to compromise privilege and power in any way. Time passed. Sedgwick noted that 'all is again at the perfect level of stagnation' (Winstanley, 1840: 273).

Further Government action, therefore, was inevitable. In 1855 a Parliamentary Commission was set up and Sedgwick was invited to be one of the new Commissioners. But the Bill drawn up to implement the reforms had missed one of the major points—that of curtailing the 'despotic and irresponsible rule' of the Heads of Colleges. Sedgwick, and three of his former colleagues on the Royal

Commission—Peacock, Herschel, and Romilly—together with Bateson their secretary, sent two strongly worded letters to the Lord Chancellor pointing out the weakness of the Bill. The Bill was accordingly modified.

The Act was passed in 1856 and put into legislation many of the recommendations of the Royal Commission. Sedgwick withdrew, however, from being one of the eight Parliamentary Commissioners, having little heart, no doubt, to create further antagonism among his colleagues, including Whewell, Master of Trinity, who had been bitterly resentful of Sedgwick's involvement with the Royal Commission. After all, the important work from Sedgwick's viewpoint, that of outlining the necessary reforms, was now done.

Prince Albert's association with Cambridge University was to be cut tragically short. In 1861 the man who had done more for the development of science and technological education than any other person in these islands, who had established the School of Mines—'a Government educational establishment for the diffusion of science generally as applied to productive industry' (Geikie, 1875, vol. II: 164–5) and the great South Kensington Museum complex, the man whose love and patronage of the arts did much to improve the quality of life in a relatively philistine society (he was a gifted composer in his own right), died of typhoid fever at the early age of 42.

Queen Victoria, at the beginning of perhaps the most celebrated widowhood in English history, sent a memorial lithograph of herself and her late husband to Sedgwick. When Sedgwick saw the portraits he confessed: 'for a few seconds, I sat down and wept like a child' (Clark and Hughes, 1890, vol. II: 375).

In the summer after Albert's death, Victoria recalled again the friendship between her husband and the elderly Yorkshire clergyman-professor who had visited them at Osborne and at Balmoral. Sedgwick, now aged 77, was summoned to Windsor, and was deeply impressed by 'the sanctity of her sorrow; by her beautiful self-possession; by her large views of her duties; by the great expansion of her love and good-will to her fellow-creatures and subjects; and by the firmness of her faith' (Clark and Hughes, 1890, vol. II: 382).

As he later recalled: 'I believe I was the first person, out of her own family, to whom she fully opened her heart, and told of her sorrows'. Talking to him as if he had been 'her elder brother': '"He had the greatest regard for you", she said, "and that is why I had a strong desire to talk with you without reserve"' (Clark and Hughes, 1890, vol. II: 391). Soon afterwards, a bound copy of Albert's speeches inscribed from 'his broken-hearted widow Victoria' arrived at Sedgwick's Cambridge rooms.

Curiously, this touching meeting, and Queen Victoria's lasting esteem for Sedgwick, was to make a small but permanent impression on far-off Dentdale.

11

Cowgill Chapel

The latter part of Adam Sedgwick's life was dominated by chronic ill-health. His absorption in his physical state became almost obsessive by the 1850s and 1860s. For a man whose constitution was strong enough to take him into his late 80s, and who was still active in public life and capable of delivering his public lectures beyond his eightieth birthday, this might seem something of a paradox. But there seems little doubt that he suffered from a number of conditions, physical as well as mental, which, at times, made life scarcely endurable.

The legacy of his 1813 breakdown, which gave him an abhorrence of sustained intellectual activity constantly returned, intensified no doubt by the bitter disappointments of the Cambrian–Silurian dispute. As he wrote in the preface of the printed text of a lecture to a local Working Men's College in 1861: 'I am incapable, at present, of any continued intellectual labour—even on so limited a plan, and connected with facts long familiar to me' (Sedgwick, 1861).

In former years, he had cherished hopes of finally getting down to the composition of a book, but it was a pipedream: 'My plan of life was to spend each Spring at some German watering place and try and write a book ... but God knows whether I shall ever be permitted to do so' (Sedgwick, 1843).

In 1865 he planned to write an autobiography; having acquired a substantial notebook, he prepared a detailed table of contents of a projected 240 page book, dividing it equally into two parts. The first, a 'Personal History' dealing with boyhood and youth, college life, his geological profession, foreign tours, reforms at the University, the Royal Family, and a little piquantly ending with a section 'under the hands of the doctor but not dead yet!' The second part was planned to deal with College and University affairs, Church affairs and connections with Norwich, and to have sections on Natural Philosophy, Moral Philosophy and Ethics, Geology, a history of the Woodwardian Museum, and his own papers and memoirs.

Each page of the notebook is numbered, and sections written, in pencil. But there are only tantalizing fragments, unrelated sections of what might have been a remarkable work; parts have been quoted, and other parts were destined to be used as part of the *Memorial*. The failure to complete the autobiography is an indication of this inertia, which increasingly overcame him and worsened as the debilitating effects of old age added to his woes.

Gout was a particularly acute affliction from his middle years. It affected him each Spring, often making life intolerable. As he wrote to Whewell, 'In society I forced myself to keep appearances; but when by myself I had such scenes of collapse and such fits of exacerbation as no one else can understand who has not been tormented by the foul working fiend of shisatic gout' (Sedgwick, 1843).

He suffered from vertigo, from stomach complaints, from bronchial trouble that forced him in the winter months to wear a respirator over his face giving him a grotesque appearance. At times, bouts of depression would overwhelm him making him believe he had wasted his abilities or had achieved nothing. They could become a challenge to his very sanity: 'My spirits are *very* low, my memory is shattered to dust—and my imaginations are no better than the dreams of a bedlamite' (Sedgwick, 1857).

Yet he retained the ability to laugh at himself and his misfortunes: 'While they try to cure one part of my old, nearly worn-out machinery they damage another. Tis something like putting new wine into old bottles; or like the work of a tinker who in patching an old kettle produces two rents in place of the old one' (Clark and Hughes, 1890, vol. II: 385–6). But the predominant mood was self-pity: 'If you knew the wretched irresolution that makes the life of a hypochondrical and gouty man, you would perhaps pity me more than blame me' (Sedgwick, 1859).

To some extent the demands of his public life sustained him. There was, as always, the annual course of lectures. By now these were something of an institution and, although they were far more discursive and anecdotal than, for example, the brilliant dissection of Lyell's *Principles* in 1831, they still had a charismatic power. Sedley Taylor, who attended Sedgwick's lectures in the late 1850s has given an entertaining account of Sedgwick in his later years:

> The sight of some fossil on the table, or of some diagram on the wall would recall the occasion on which he found the one or noted down the memoranda for the other. 'I was taking a geological excursion with my

dear friend—long since dead, gentlemen, like most of my contemporaries'; and off he would go, recounting the 'glorious time we had together' with an exuberance of cheery reminiscence, a vivid picturesqueness of description, and a homely raciness of language, the impression of which remains with me still. Then, after an apologetic 'But this is all by the way gentlemen, this is all by the way' he would abruptly fall on his assistant with 'Where is that fossil? Eh, what do you say? Oh! ah! yes!' and then launch out into a description of the animal of whose body the fossil in question had once formed part: 'a very queer old fellow, gentlemen,' just as though he had met him a short time before. (Clark and Hughes, 1890, vol. II: 488)

And yet, in the fiftieth course of lectures in 1868, at the age of 83, he could reveal a remarkable intellectual vitality. Notwithstanding his frequent outbursts against Darwin and the *Vestiges*, he was prepared to re-examine his own position on the fundamental question of the antiquity of man:

Gentlemen, I have hitherto, in the successive courses of lectures delivered from this chair as Woodwardian Professor, always maintained, in opposition to my distinguished friend Sir Charles Lyell, that man, geologically speaking, is of very recent appearance on the earth. But during the last Long Vacation, I have gone again over the whole evidence, including much new matter of great importance, and am now bound to admit that I can no longer maintain the position I have hitherto held. I must freely admit that a man is of a far higher antiquity than that which I have hitherto assigned to him. (Clark and Hughes, 1890, vol. II: 440)

—but going on, perhaps inevitably, to denounce the 'degrading hypothesis' of the Darwinians.

Clark and Hughes record how the annual course of lectures seemed to revitalise him, noting his own remark ' they keep me alive'.

By now, the tall, white-haired figure was regarded with almost universal affection in Cambridge, even from those who felt his views outmoded.

He was also sustained by the warm relationship he had with some of his young, mostly female admirers, his nieces (particularly his beloved Isabella who constantly cared for him and nursed him in his closing years) and daughters of colleagues or acquaintances. The more loquacious style of Victorian letters occasionally reveals a remarkable frankness of feeling in certain of these letters, which perhaps moves beyond the conventional fatherly affection and tenderness so typical of Sedgwick. A letter to Miss Maud Pagett, daughter of Sir George Pagett, Regent Professor at Cambridge, in 1866 is perhaps an example:

> I am now far too old and clumsy to climb mountains, and I must be content to remain below. And, my darling, I shall not be allowed to remain anywhere very long. But while God spares my life I hope he will teach me to love young people like yourself, and I do not want much teaching, it seems to me quite natural. I can't help knowing this. So to keep me alive I send 100 kisses to you and to your visitors—a hundred to each—and each kiss as long as a pistol shot, a good (—) smack that might be heard from Plas Isa to the top of Penmaenmawr.
> Ever my darling,
> Adam Sedgwick. (Sedgwick, 1869b)

However, it was the affairs of Dentdale that came to preoccupy him increasingly. Although rail travel now made the journey to Yorkshire very much quicker and easier, each year made him less capable of the physical ordeals of any mode of travel.

When, in 1859, after a prolonged illness, John Sedgwick died, Adam Sedgwick was delighted to discover that his nephew, Richard, after an initial hesitation would now accept his father's post of Vicar of Dent;

> his affection of early life came back so strong, that he wished to be put in nomination; and I have no doubt of his election to his father's house and office. For the remaining years of my life I shall not therefore, be without a home in this valley. Rather I shall have two homes in it—one at the Parsonage, and the other at the cottage where, I trust, my sister and niece will live. (Sedgwick, 1859).

True to form, the Sidesmen elected Richard Sedgwick Vicar of Dent, but events did not run quite as smoothly. In 1864 Richard Sedgwick had a mental breakdown, and Sedgwick had to assume responsibility for 'my poor unhappy nephew who is now a lunatic', his wife and eight children, a further drain on his time and limited financial resources.

Another event also drew him to Dentdale. In 1837 Sedgwick had laid the foundation stone of a small chapel at Cowgill, Upper Dentdale, close to the point where some 20 years earlier his sister had started a Sunday school to help combat the lawlessness and lack of moral instruction among the inhabitants of the area at the time of the decay of the social fabric in the Dale.

The policy of building new churches to keep the minds of the poor away from Chartist feeling, is one more readily associated with urban areas than rural (Marshall, 1973; 152), but the success of the new little chapel seemed assured from the response to this new home of religion:

Cowgill Chapel

Cowgill Chapel.

The day was glorious, the face of nature beautiful, and all parties in good humour and charity. About seven hundred mountaineers, including nearly two hundred Sunday school children and about one hundred strangers, some of whom came from the distance of twenty miles, made a curious mixed procession in the wild glen where the little chapel is now rising from the ground. It is built upon the solid rock which forms the bed of a mountain stream that washes the churchyard side, and over which the waters descend in long succession of rapids and falls; and it will be surrounded by birch, mountain-ash and other wild trees of the country. I trust God will bless the undertaking which begins so smilingly. We began by making the rocks echo back the old hundredth Psalms; my brother read one or two short prayers from our liturgy; Mr Wilson made a short address; I handled the trowel, and laid the stone, and then addressed my countrymen, after which we again uncurled ourselves into a long string to the tune of *God Save the King* and the strangers, school-children, and some others went down to Dent and had cold meat and coffee at the old parsonage. My sister made thirty-six gallons of coffee in a brewing-vessel.   (Clark and Hughes, 1890, vol. I: 487–8).

Unfortunately, though the documents relating to the foundation and the consecration of the chapel were sent to the Bishop of Ripon (as head of the Diocese), nearly 30 years afterwards the Trustees of the Chapel, of whom Sedgwick was one, discovered to their horror that the documents had never been properly registered. After some discussion, the matter was taken up with the Church authorities, who promptly agreed to take the necessary steps. The Trustees thought no more about the matter and did not even bother to check the details of the award as it was printed. Their distress can only be imagined, therefore, when they discovered that the registration directed that the ancient name of their Chapel at Cowgill be changed to Kirkthwaite.

It would seem that some well meaning ecclesiastical official had determined that the name 'Cowgill' was uncouth and had registered the Chapel in the name of the nearby hamlet of Kirthwaite, and added insult to injury by adding an unncessary 'k'. Few things insult the dignity of a Dalesman more than misnaming a place in the dale of his birth. The name Cowgill, was, in fact, steeped in history. As Sedgwick wrote: 'Again, the Cogill or Coegill (we should much prefer this orthography to that of Cowgill) is not an obscure ravine and watercourse in Kirthwaite. Its name, variably spelt, appears in the old Boundary Rolls. It gives the name, Cogill Wold, to a high tract upon the mountains on the north side of Kirthwaite' (Sedgwick, 1868: 15).

The Trustees, with Sedgwick as their spokesman incorporated their objections in a 'Memorial' to the Ecclesiastical Commissioners, which was sent to them in December 1866 and which ended with the 'loyal and earnest prayer' that their Award should be modified so that 'its verbal contradictions may disappear and the errors in the orthography of the word Kirthwaite may be corrected, that the name Cowgill be fully retained; that its District be named (as it was named in the first three successive Presentations) the Chaperly of Cowgill'. But the Commissioners wrote back to protest that they had 'No power of altering the title under which a District may have been legally created' (Sedgwick, 1868).

Sedgwick determined not to let the matter end there. He decided to have the *Memorial* privately printed and circulated among the Statesmen, and others who had contributed towards the cost of building and endowing the chapel. He also decided to add to the *Memorial* (in the usual Sedgwickian manner) an extended Preface and no less than six separate appendices, largely dictated to his servant (his eyes now troubling him so much, and the gout affecting his ability to hold a pen), writing was an increasing labour to him. These appendices cover much of the autobiographical material already quoted, and with essays on the climate, history, customs, dialect and farming of the Dale, form, as has been suggested, a unique record of Dentdale life. It was published, 'the child of my old age, dressed in an old fashioned dress of a child of the Dales' (i.e. green), in 1868, when Sedgwick was 83.

Sedgwick later described the extraordinary chain of events that brought the little pamphlet into the hands of Queen Victoria, who, recalling her old friend, acted with surprising swiftness:

> One of the daughters of the late Bishop Stanley asked me for a copy of my Dent pamphlet for her sister-in-law at the Deanery of Westminster, then she asked me for another copy which, when she afterwards visited Windsor Castle, she spoke to the Queen about, who, to my great surprise, communicated with me, through General Gray, and asked for a copy of my pamphlet. Of course I complied, with all loyalty, with her Majesty's wishes. She reacted, as General Gray informed me by letter, that the name of Cowgill Chapel ought never to have been changed and that she was willing to take any steps to undo the wrong. Through General Gray the Queen applied to the Archbishop of York upon the subject, and the General advised me to send a copy of my pamphlet to his Grace.   (Sedgwick, 1869).

As Sedgwick confessed:

> I declare that while I was dictating my pamphlet I should as soon have thought of directing it, by the Book Post, to the Planet Neptune as Balmoral! Had I known that it would be read by my Sovereign I should not have dared to write about the old tailor or wig-maker, and about the 'night-sittings' and the 'crying out' in Dent. And it would not have been half so spicey as it is.   (Clark and Hughes, 1890, vol.II: 437–8)

Doubtless Victoria enjoyed the episodes of tailor, wig-maker, and 'night-sittings' every bit as much as a modern reader and one can only remain thankful that Sedgwick did write for his fellow Dalesmen rather than his Sovereign.

It was discovered that an Act of Parliament was required to change the name. But the Queen desired it—so the ponderous machinery of Government creaked into action. Gladstone himself took the matter up. The Archbishop introduced the Bill in the Lords and the Commons saw it through. In July 1869 the Act went through Parliament and the 'District Chaperly of Kirkthwaite' was now the 'District Chapel of Cowgill'. Rarely has the mighty hammer of Parliamentary legislation cracked such a tiny nut of a little church's name. Yet it represented something far more than a little local dispute; it is an enduring symbol of the very real affection and respect a widowed Queen had for an ageing scholar and family friend, a remarkable token of royal gratitude.

Although now sick and ill (his many other ailments were increased by an accidental fall when rashly visiting Hell Cauldron, a rocky gorge in the river near Gib's Hall, Dent, with grand-nephew and nieces, at the tender age of 83; he was lame for some months after-

Adam Sedgwick

wards), he still had bursts of the old fire and energy. He encouraged Isabella to take a well earned holiday in Italy in 1869 and was able to attend, in the same year, a Golden Jubilee Meeting of the Philosophical Society, as their only surviving founder member.

And he was still able to lecture, attracting the usual large audiences.

> Yesterday the petticoats mustered full twenty, and the pantaloon-wearing bipeds about thirty. When I had done my regular lecture of an hour and a quarter, I went down to our basement floor to show the big skeletons, and bones that are too big to be brought up to my lecture room and there I gave a kind of second lecture. So that I did not get back to my rooms before 2 pm. I *was* a little tired... (Clark and Hughes, 1890, vol. II: 450)

This is remarkable not only for the extraordinary stamina of an 84-year-old, but for the large proportion of women in his audience at a time when women undergraduates were still unknown at the University—Girton College was founded only in 1869, and only came to Cambridge in 1871.

In 1870 he had sufficient energy to work on a little sequel to the *Memorial*, called rather dully, the *Supplement to the Memorial*. This again is a fine pamphlet, recounting the details of the successful outcome of the Queen's intervention, and again adding marvellous details of personal and Dales history. It was written, as the *Memorial* had been written, for his friends, 'a pleasant gossip with my brother Dalesman'; yet it has a valedictory quality. He was 85, time was running out, yet it has a vividness and a photographic clarity, that of an old man's memory, which gives it an astonishing freshness.

Recalling a favourite ramble, he urges his countrymen to relive the joy he had experienced in a magnificent landscape:

> Many times when a schoolboy I have gone, on a half-holiday, with my class-fellows to those Firbank hills; and we could select for ourselves the points of view which at once brought before our sight five distinct valleys which seemed to unite in a great basin or central depression at our feet, in the upper part of which the tower of Sedbergh Church was seen in the distance. Down four of these valleys the waters descend into the central basin. Through the fifth they make their final escape through the lovely scenery of the Lower Lune. Should this note reach the sight of any of my countrymen or countrywomen, I exhort them to walk to the top of one of these Firbank hills (a very easy task), and warm their hearts by gazing over this cluster of noble Dales, among which Providence placed the land of their Fathers, and the home of their childhood.

The *Supplement* ends with a farewell, an ending of 'this country gossip':

> Old Time for many a long year has, with his inaudible and never-weary foot, been following my path, and allowing me to walk cheerfully before him. But he presses hard upon me now, and I know full well that he may at any moment tread upon my heel and tell me that my life journey upon earth is at an end. Let me, however, in these parting words speak to my old friends no long under a figure, but in the simplest words I can call to mind. We all know full well that our life is uncertain, and that its end is one of our Maker's secrets. But this, at least, is certain, that an old man has but a small portion of this world's life before him. To acknowledge such a simple truth is one thing; but to bring it home to the heart is another; and the two, alas! are often far asunder. (Sedgwick, 1870)

He was only to visit Dent once more, in the summer of 1870, when he spoke to the village schoolchildren from a stone-bench in the school yard. One wonders what they must have made of the strange old man.

The last three years of Sedgwick's life was a time when illness and disability were barely kept at bay. He was still able to lecture in 1870—his fifty-second course—but this was the last time. He continued to work in the Museum, expanding the collection, cataloguing. He carried out his duties at Norwich as well as he was able. He could still get out for the odd walk, or even drive; but for a man who had been so energetic and active, old age meant isolation and loneliness, being confined to his College rooms, unable to read by candlelight, writing with extreme difficulty except with an amanuensis, suffering the indignity of prostate trouble that caused him to require help even with bodily functions. 'No-one thinks of calling on such a crabbed, half-blind, half-deaf old dotard as myself'.

Above all, he missed Dent, realizing that he was too old and ill to return, giving even more generously than usual to the poor and needy, for example at Christmas, than when he had been able to be present.

His last work—at the age of 87—was written in Norwich and was a *Preface* to the great *Catalogue of Cambrian and Silurian fossils* prepared by his old colleague J. W. Salter, who had committed suicide in the Thames three years earlier. It was a scientific work of some importance, outlining his own work in the field of Cambrian geology, and his career at the University. Typically it ends with a statement about the 'Great First Cause' and it indicates that even at the very end of his life Sedgwick had lost little of his intellectual power and insight. It was dictated to Isabella who later recorded that

Adam Sedgwick

the conclusion, 'some grave and solemn words to say, words, which he felt would be the last he should ever address to the public', was dictated at such speed that: 'I wrote as rapidly as I could, but it was difficult to keep up with the rapid flow of words; sentence after sentence was spoken with scarcely a pause for thought' (Clark and Hughes, 1890, vol. II: 473).

Early in 1873, after a short illness, in Norwich, and close to his beloved Isabella, Adam Sedgwick died. He was 88. Amongst the many messages of condolence was a telegram from the Queen: 'I am deeply grieved to hear of the death of our kind old friend, Professor Sedgwick. He was a most valued friend of the dear Prince. Pray let me have some details' (Clark and Hughes, 1890, vol. II: 462).

He was buried in Trinity College Chapel, close to his old friend, colleague and sparring-partner William Whewell, under a simple marble tablet bearing nothing but his name and the years of his Vice Mastership. More elaborate memorials were prepared in Norwich Cathedral where a stained glass window was dedicated; in Dent Church in the form of a fine and simple tablet written by Professor Selwyn; in the Woodwardian Museum, developed into extensive and noble premises and renamed the Sedgwick Museum in 1904, where a splendid statue now stands; and in Dent main street following a collection among his native Dalesmen, the massive granite fountain where we began.

Of the many deeply felt tributes and resonant oratory uttered to the memory of Sedgwick in the University, in the learned Societies and elsewhere, none captured the essence of Adam Sedgwick the man better than that of Professor Selwyn in support of the proposal, at a public meeting in Cambridge in 1873, to name a proposed new Geological Museum the Sedgwick Museum:

> Let me say he was a most *primitive* man—of the solid ancient rock of humanity. He appears like a great boulder-stone of granite, such as he describes, transported from Shap Fell over the hills of Yorkshire, dropped here in our lowland country, and here fixed for life; primitive in his name, Adam; primitive in his nature; in his rugged noble simplicity; a dalesman of the north; primitive in his love of all ancient good things and ways; primitive in his love of nature and of his native rock from which he was hewn; primitive in his loyalty to truth, and hatred of everything that was false and mean; a heart if ever there was one, that 'turned upon the poles of truth'. (Clark and Hughes, 1890, vol. II: 483).

12

The interpreter of a landscape

From the perspective of just over a century since Adam Sedgwick's death, what is it that to us in the late twentieth century seems to be of most enduring significance? His achievements, during a long and active life, were numerous and in different fields.

There was his involvement with the community of his birth which led, albeit indirectly, to a piece of fine social history which is of more than local significance. There was also his achievement as a geologist, an achievement soundly based on a brilliant field-technique that must undoubtedly make him one of the finest empirical geologists of all time. Significant, too, was his contribution, in the University, through the Geological Society, the Cambridge Philosophical Society and through other Societies, to the development of Geology as a scientific discipline and to its study and teaching. There was, too, his contribution to the idea of a University based on broad, humane, liberal ideas, and the moral and political courage that helped, with royal patronage, to turn those ideals into reality.

In all these things, including the Darwinian controversy, Adam Sedgwick was at the centre of stage. His combination of absolute integrity and liberal radicalism place him in the mainstream of the great English radical tradition of the nineteenth and twentieth centuries, a tradition stretching from Cobbett to Orwell which, in its constant protest at the abuses of power and privilege, has helped establish much that is precious and valuable in the communal life of these islands.

Over the single most important scientific event of the nineteenth century, the publication of the *Origin of Species*, he opposed

Darwin, but not, as is usually suggested, out of mere ignorance or innate conservatism, but because, more acutely than those around him, he foresaw the emergence of an inhumane materialism—'he feared that the specious plausibility of its all-embracing naturalistic 'development' would undermine that sense of personal responsibility that he believed was basic to the nature of man in society' (Rudwick, 1975)—a fear with which, after two World Wars and a Hiroshima we can have more sympathy.

As Cannon argues, moreover, were it not for the excellent case presented against Darwin's theories by men of the calibre of Sedgwick and Whewell—the 'Christian Romantics'—Darwin would not have been challenged to present so complete and convincing a case for Evolution (Cannon, 1976).

Remarkable, too, were his gifts as a teacher—the brilliant lectures, the dazzling oratory, the skill with language and the ability to convey, to his audience, something of his own extraordinary personality, the humour, the compassion, the immense vitality, the tremendous zest for life, the enthusiasm for creation's splendours. Yet this extrovert nature disguised an obsessive and almost morbid hypochondria, and inner loneliness and that inability to sustain a prolonged intellectual effort that cost the world a major scientific work on the scale of a *Siluria* or *Principles of Geology* and which ultimately denied him the recognition of his single most important scientific achievement—the resolution of the Cambrian issue—by the scientific world at large, a recognition that clearly his ambitious nature craved. To some extent his constant public activity was a psychological necessity for him, a recognition of that identity as a scholar and a scientist which he had been for so long establishing.

His third career, that of a clergyman, must be seen to be subservient to his work as a teacher and geologist; in matters theological he was not an original thinker, and his sermons though noted for sincerity of feeling and a certain Low Church directness, were not in any way remarkable.

No story perhaps illustrates the engaging blend of self-deprecating humour and professional dedication so typical of Sedgwick than the one he told against himself when in North Wales. After a long day in the hills, returning 'dog-tired', Sedgwick paused by the roadside and began hammering away at some fossils. A fashionable lady passed, asking Sedgwick about the district, and about which Sedgwick, of course, informed her with his usual courteousness.

'She thanked me for my information, and added 'Poor man, you must find this very hard work'. 'Yes, indeed I do' I replied; whereupon she

The interpreter of a landscape

Adam Sedgwick in later life.

took out her purse and gave me a shilling. Next evening, to my great amusement, she came to dine at the house where I was staying. I recognised her at once, but she did not know me in my altered dress. She was visiting Wales for the first time, and was full of enthusiasm for the scenery and the people. 'They are so obliging and so communicative', she said; 'only yesterday I had a long conversation with an old man who was breaking stones on the road. He told me all I wanted to know, and was so civil that I gave him a shilling.' I could not resist the pleasure of saying, 'Yes Ma'am you did, and here it is'   (Clark and Hughes, 1980, vol. II: 574)

These things endure; yet perhaps the most neglected aspect of Sedgwick's work of all is, curiously, that which should be most accessible to us, and that is his writing. It was a characteristic feature of many of the great geologists of the nineteenth century that they were also

Adam Sedgwick

masters of the literary craft—one thinks of the fine prose of men like Playfair, Lyell, Phillips, Hugh Miller and Archibald Geikie. To some extent the quality of a man's literary style reflects the mind and personality of the writer himself, and many great works of science, for example *The Voyage of the Beagle* or the *Origin* itself, are also great works of literature for their inherent literary as well as scientific qualities. It would be surprising, therefore, if Sedgwick's brilliant gifts of oratory, so carefully noted by people like Richard Wilton, weren't reflected in his prose.

Many of Sedgwick's major scientific papers, forgotten in the yellowing pages of Journals and Transactions in the archives and cellars of libraries, still have considerable inherent interest, reflecting as they do the original perceptions of a scientific discovery, the first interpretation of phenomena that have since become standard geological knowledge. Take, for example, one particular small, but significant discovery of Sedgwick's, the line of what is now known as the Dent Fault, which is part of the great fault system that separates the Silurian rocks of the Lake District from the Carboniferous rocks of the Central Pennines, forming the dramatic pass of Barbondale.

In his paper 'Introduction to the general structure of the Cumbrian Mountains', published in the *Transactions of the Geological Society* in 1835, Sedgwick describes the stages by which he unravelled this Fault system:

> I once imagined that this great fault ranged through the neighbourhood of Kirkby Lonsdale and Farlton Knot and there terminated. It is unquestionable that the lines of dislocation do range in the direction here indicated (as is proved by the position of the limestone of Kirkby Lonsdale bridge, and the still more remarkable position of the limestone between Casterton and Barbon); but after several subsequent visits to the neighbourhood I found that the local branch of the Craven Fault ranged along the line of junction of the central chain which skirts the Cumbrian system, passing along the south flank of Casterton Low Fell up Barbondale, then across the valley of Dent, through the upper part of the valley of Sedbergh, and along the flank of Bowfell and Wildboar Fell, and the ridge between Mallerstang and Ravenstone Dale; and that along the whole of this line there are enormous and most complex dislocations; and it became a question of some consequence to determine the further range and nature of the great Craven Fault.

The fascination of this extract lies in the reader's share in the excitement of discovery; the stages in elucidation are made clear 'I once imagined', 'I found' and, the discoveries then made 'after several subsequent visits' posing further difficulties and riddles 'a question of some consequence'. Thus we share the process of scientific dis-

The interpreter of a landscape

covery, the interest in 'the remarkable' position of the limestone, the sense of wonder, which is, or should be, the essence of science. The language is simple, direct and non-technical, avoiding the jargon and specialized terminology which, perhaps inevitably, makes most later geological work unreadable by the layman.

One of Sedgwick's greatest prose works, now totally neglected, is the Five great 'Letters' to Wordsworth on the geology of the Lake District, deliberately written for a lay audience, and published with Wordsworth's Guide in John Hudson's *Complete Guide to the Lakes*. It was a work which prompted one William Pearson of Crossthwaite to confess he had 'read over and over for the peculiar interest they excite in all lovers of our beautiful district' (Pearson, 1855).

Again, much of the interest in these 'Letters' (why Sedgwick had chosen to use such a curious literary form for these essays is not clear; his good friend Thomas Gough went as far as to suggest that Sedgwick need not add the usual personal 'signing off' at the end of each letter) lies in the fact that Sedgwick could describe the geological facts from first-hand discovery and experience. They also demonstrate a rich power of metaphor and a rare ability to express difficult abstract ideas in vivid, earthy images. Take the Second Letter which, perhaps, must be unrivalled in the whole literature of geology for the splendour of its imaginative sweep:

> My present object is to convey some notion of the structure of the great mountain masses, and to show how the several parts are fitted one to another. This can only be done after great labour. The cliffs where the rocks are laid bare by the sea, the clefts and fissures in the hills and valleys, the deep grooves through which the waters flow—all must in turn be examined; and out of such seeming confusion order will at length appear. We must, in imagination, sweep off the drifted matter that clogs the surface of the ground; we must suppose all the covering of moss and heath and wood to be torn away from the sides of the mountains, and the green mantle that lies near their feet to be lifted up; we may see the muscular integuments and sinews and bones of our mother Earth, and so judge of the parts played by each of them during those old convulsive movements whereby her limbs were contorted and drawn up into their present positions. (Sedgwick, 1853b).

The imagery here, so beautifully precise, is that of a poet.

It takes another poet, the Cumbrian poet Norman Nicholson, to give precise definition to the kind of insight given by the geologist into landscape interpretation: 'To look at the scenery without trying to understand the rock is like listening to poetry in an unknown language. You hear the beauty but you miss the meaning' (N.

Nicholson, 1963).

The 'Letters on the Geology of the Lake District' and many of the geological papers are, in essence, interpretations of landscape and as such can be seen within a tradition of Romantic painting, poetry and topography of the late eighteenth and early nineteenth centuries. It is no accident that the 'discovery' of the Lakeland mountains by Pococke, Grey, Gilpin, West, Wordsworth and others was followed, almost directly, by Jonathan Otley and Adam Sedgwick's brilliant exposition of the underlying rock structure—or 'language' of the rocks.

This growing awareness of landscape, developed and encouraged by Sedgwick through the widening network of Scientific Societies, Mechanics' Institutes and adult education classes, leads directly to what is known as the Outdoor Movement—the Holiday Fellowship, Countryside Holidays Association, the Youth Hostels Association, Ramblers' Association, Naturalists' Unions, Workers Education Associations. It is reflected in the legislation which has lead to the creation of National Parks, Nature Reserves, Long Distance Footpaths and all the many modern agencies of conservation and education.

Adam Sedgwick, lifelong fell-walker and rambler, were he to see the descendants of his Manchester artisans, his Tynemouth colliers, his Kendal amateurs and Cambridge bluestockings, in their thousands, with rucksack and boots, out on the fells when the spring snow still lies fresh and white on the tops, learning to read the language of his native fells, he would be truly delighted.

References and Bibliography

Allen, D. E. 1976. *The Naturalist in Britain.* London
Anonymous. 1821. John Dawson, Obituary. *The Lonsdale Magazine* (2) **13**.
Babbage, C. 1830. *Reflections on the decline of science in England.* London.
Barlow, N. 1974. *Darwin and Henslow; the growth of an idea.* London.
Bonney, T. G. 1897. Adam Sedgwick. *Dictionary of National Biography* **25**: 179–183.
Booth, C. C. 1970. John Dawson 1734–1820. *British Medical Journal* **5728**: 171–173.
Buckley, J. H. 1960. *Tennyson: the growth of a poet's mind.* Cambridge, Mass.
Cannon, W. F. 1960a. The problem of miracles in the 1830s. *Victorian Studies* **4**: 5–32.
——. 1960b. The uniformatarian-catastrophist debate. *Isis* **51**: 38–46.
——. 1964. Scientists and broad churchmen; an early Victorian network. *Journal of British Studies* **4**: 65–68.
——. 1976. The Whewell-Darwin controversy. *Journal of the Geological Society of London* **132**: 377–384.
Chambers, R. 1844. *Vestiges of the natural history of creation.* Edinburgh.
Clark, J. W. & Hughes, T. M. 1890. *The life and letters of the Reverend Adam Sedgwick.* Cambridge. 2 vols. (Reprint by Gregg Press a subsidiary of Avebury Publishing Company, Amersham, Bucks).
Clarke, H. L. & Weech, W. N. 1925. *The history of Sedbergh school 1525–1925.* Sedbergh.
Darwin, C. 1859. *On the origin of the species by means of natural selection.* London.
Darwin, F. 1887. *The life and letters of Charles Darwin.* London. 2 vols.
Davies, G. L. 1969. *The Earth in decay.* London.
De Beer, G. R. 1974 Editor. *Charles Darwin and Thomas Henry Huxley. Autobiographies.* Oxford.
Erikson, E. 1980. *Childhood and society.* New York.
Fenton, C. L. & Fenton, M. A. 1945. *The story of the great geologists.* New York.
Geikie, A. 1875. *The life of Sir Roderick Impey Murchison.* London. 2 vols.
——. 1897. *The founders of geology.* London.
Gillispie, C. C. 1951. *Genesis and geology.* Cambridge, Mass.
Glick, T. E. 1974. *The comparative reception of Darwinism.* Austin, Texas.
Gough, T. 1853. Letter to Sedgwick. Manuscript, Cambridge University Library.
Gunther, R. W. T. 1937. *Early science in Cambridge.* Oxford.

Hall, A. R. 1969. *The Cambridge Philosophical Society. A history 1819–1969.* Cambridge.

Himmelfarb, G. 1959. *Darwin and the Darwinian revolution.* London.

Howarth, O. J. R. 1931. *The British Association for the Advancement of Science—a retrospect.* London.

Howitt, M. 1840. *Hope on, Hope ever!* London.

Howitt, W. 1838. *The rural life of England.* London.

Hudson, J. 1843. *A complete guide to the Lakes ... with Mr Wordsworth's description of the scenery of the country, etc. and three letters on the geology of the Lake District by Professor Sedgwick.* Kendal. (4th ed., 1853: 5th ed., 1859).

Hughes, T. McK. 1883. Adam Sedgwick. *Proceedings of the Yorkshire Geological Society* **8**: 255–268.

Hull, D. L. 1974. *Darwin and his critics.* Cambridge, Mass.

Huxley, T. H. 1893. *Evolution and ethics.* London.

James, D. F. 1969. Adam Sedgwick and his Kendal disciples. *Magazine of the Kendal Museum* **8**.

Kelly, T. 1970. *A history of adult education in Great Britain.* Liverpool.

Kendal Natural History and Scientific Society. Minute Books. Cumbria County Council archives, Kendal.

Lyell, C. 1830–1833. *Principles of geology.* London. 3 vols.

Lyon, K. 1978. Whernside Manor: a house with a tale to tell. *Dalesman's Yorkshire Annual* 1979.

Mandlebaum, M. 1971. *History, man and reason.* Baltimore.

Marshall, D. 1973. *Industrial England, 1776–1851.* London.

Miller, H. 1841. *The Old Red Sandstone.* London.

Millhauser, M. 1959. *Just before Darwin, Robert Chambers and Vestiges.* Middletown, Conn.

Morrell, J. B. 1971. Individualism and the structure of British science in 1830. *Historical studies in the physical sciences* 3: 183–204.

——. 1977. Science and the universities. *History of Science* **15**: 145–152.

Murchison, R. I. 1839. *The Silurian System.* London.

——. 1854. *Siluria.* London.

——. 1869a. Letter to A. Sedgwick. Dated 6 January and not posted. Manuscript, Cambridge University Library.

——. 1869b. Letter to A. Sedgwick. Dated 7 January. Manuscript, Cambridge University Library.

Nicholson, C. 1861. *The annals of Kendal.* Kendal.

Nicholson, N. 1963. *A portrait of the Lakes.* London.

Orange, A. D. 1973. *Philosophers and provincials.* York.

Paley, W. 1802. *Natural theology.* London.

Pearson, W. 1855. Letter to A. Sedgwick. Dated 13 October. Manuscript, Cambridge University Library.

Phenix, P. H. 1964. *Realms of meaning.* New York.

Phillips, J. 1844. *William Smith.* London.

——. 1873. Sedgwick. *Nature* **7**: 257–259.

Porter, R. 1973. The industrial revolution and the rise of the science of geology. *In* M. Teich and R. Young. Editors. *Changing perspectives in the history of science.* London, pp. 320–343.

——. 1977a. *The making of geology.* Cambridge.

——. 1977b. The natural science tripos and the Cambridge School of Geology 1850–1914. Unpublished typescript.

References and Bibliography

Pound, R. 1973. *Albert—a biography of the Prince Consort.* London.
Raistrick, A. 1950. Sedgwick and Dentdale. *Country and Travel*
——. 1967. *Old Yorkshire Dales.* Newton Abbot.
——. 1968. *The Pennine Dales.* London.
Ravetz, J. R. 1971. *Scientific knowledge and its social problems.* Oxford.
Rennie, [G], Brown, [R], & Shirreff, [J] 1794. *General view of the agricultural of the West Riding of Yorkshire.* London.
Romanes, G. 1878. *A candid examination of theism.* London.
Rothblatt, S. 1968. *The revolution of the dons.* London.
Rudwick, M. J. S. 1972. *The meaning of fossils.* London.
——. 1974. Roderick Impey Murchison. *Dictionary of Scientific Biography* **9**: 582–585.
——. 1975. Adam Sedgwick. *Dictionary of Scientific Biography* **12**: 275–279.
——. 1976. Levels of disagreement in the Sedgwick-Murchison controversy. *Journal of the Geological Society of London* **132**: 373–376.
Sedgwick, A. No date. Lecture notebooks. Sedgwick Museum, Cambridge.
——. No date. Notebook containing fragments of autobiography. Manuscript, Cambridge University Library.
——. 1821. *A syllabus of a course of lectures of geology.* Cambridge.
——. [1829]. On the geological relations and internal structure of the Magnesian Limestone, *etc. Transactions of the Geological Society of London* (2) **3**: 37–124. (Read November 17 1826, April 30, May 18, 1827, March 7, 1828).
——. 1831. Presidential address to the Geological Society. *Proceedings of the Geological Society of London* **1**: 281–316.
——. 1834. *Discourse on the studies of the University.* 2nd ed. Cambridge.
——. 1835a. Remarks on the structure of large mineral masses *etc. Transactions of the Geological Society of London* (2) **3**: 461–486. (Read March 11 1835).
——. 1835b. Introduction to the general structure of the Cumbrian Mountains, *etc. Transactions of the Geological Society of London* (2) **4**: 47–68. (Read January 5 1831).
——. 1842. Report on lecture to the British Association. *Manchester Guardian,* 29 June, supplement.
——. 1843. Letter to W. Whewell, 15 September. Manuscript, Trinity College, Cambridge.
——. 1850. *Discourse on the studies of the University of Cambridge.* 5th ed. Cambridge.
——. 1852. On the classification and nomenclature of the Lower Palaeozoic rocks of England and Wales. *Quarterly Journal of the Geological Society of London* **8**: 136–168.
——. 1853a. On a proposed separation of the so-called Caradoc Sandstone into two distinct groups. *Quarterly Journal of the Geological Society of London* **9**: 215–230
——. 1853b. *See* Hudson, J. 1843.
——. 1854. On the May Hill sandstone and the Palaeozoic system of England. *Philosophical Magazine* (4) **8**: 472–506.
——. 1857. Letter to Lady Affleck. Dated 9 August.
——. 1859. Letter to Lady Affleck. Dated 10 February. Manuscript, Cambridge University Library.
[——]. 1860. Letter on the *Origin of Species. The Spectator,* 24 March: 285; 7 April: 344.
——. 1861. *A lecture on the strata near Cambridge and the Fens of the Bedford Level.* Cambridge.

———. 1862. Letter to Robert Baines Armstrong. Dated 20 May. Manuscript, Cumbria County Archives, Kendal.

———. 1868. *A memorial by the Trustees of Cowgill Chapel.* Cambridge.

———. 1869a. Letter to Murchison. Dated 2 January. Manuscript, Cambridge University Library.

———. 1869b. Letter to Miss Maud Padgett. Dated 6 January. Manuscript, Cambridge University Library.

———. 1869c. Letter to Murchison. Dated 20 January 1869. Manuscript, Cambridge University Library.

———. 1869d. Letter to Murchison. Dated 21 February. Manuscript, Cambridge University Library.

———. 1870. *Supplement to the Memorial by the Trustees of Cowgill Chapel.* Cambridge.

———. 1873. Preface. *In* J. W. Salter. *A catalogue of the collection of Cambrian and Silurian fossils contained in the Geological Museum of the University of Cambridge.* Cambridge.

——— & Murchison, R. I. 1836. On the Silurian and Cambrian systems exhibiting the order in which the older sedimentary strata succeed each other in England and Wales. *Report of the British Association* 1835: 59–61.

——— & ———. 1839a. [Classification of the older rocks of Devon and Cornwall]. *Proceedings of the Geological Society of London* **3**: 121–123.

——— & ———. 1839b. Classification of the older stratified rocks of Devonshire and Cornwall. *Philosophical Magazine* (3) **14**: 241–260.

——— & ———. 1840. On the physical structure of Devonshire, *etc. Transactions of the Geological Society of London* (2) **5**: 633–704.

Smiles, S. 1859. *Self help.* London.

Swinnerton, H. H. 1960. *Fossils.* London.

Tennyson, A. 1847. *The Princess.* London.

———. 1850. *In memorian.* London.

Thackray, J. C. 1976. The Murchison-Sedgwick controversy. *Journal of the Geological Society of London* **132**: 367–372.

Wells, A. K. 1938. *Outline of historical geology.* London.

Wilton, R. 1849a. Letter to George Maxine of Doncaster. Dated 6 November.

———. 1849b. Diaries and letters. Sedgwick Museum, Cambridge.

Winstanley, D. A. 1940. *Early Victorian Cambridge.* Cambridge.

Woodward, H. H. 1907. *The history of the Geological Society of London.* London.

———. 1911. *The story of geology.* London.

Woodward, J. 1695. *Natural history of the Earth.* London.

Wordsworth, W. 1810. *See* Hudson, J. 1843.

———. 1814. *The excursion.* London.

Young, M. B. 1967. *Richard Wilton—a forgotten Victorian.* Cambridge.

Index

Note: bold figures indicate illustrations
Affleck, Lady, 83
Agassiz, Jean Louis R. (1807–73), 102, 109
Ainger, William (1783–1840), 39, 50, 55
Airey, George (1801–92), 90, 115
Albert, Prince Consort (1819–1861), 112, **113,** 114–121, 132
Alps, 68
Apostles, The, 88
Armstrong, Robert B. (1784–1869), 39

Babbage, Charles (1792–1871), 68, 90, 91
Barbondale Pass, 72, 136
Barrande, Joachim (1799–1883), 78, 79
Bateman, W. (1746–82), 6
Bateson, John, 119, 120
Beagle, HMS
   Darwin, 102
   Voyage, 136
Beaumont, L. Elie de (1798–1874), 60, 104
Birkbeck, George, 94, 95
Bland, Miles (1784–1867), 38, 39, 46, 49
Bracken, Dr., 40
Brewster, David (1781–1868), 90, 91
British Association for the Advancement of Science
   Formation, 70, 71, 91–4
   Meetings, Cambridge, 92; Dublin, 70; Glasgow, 82; Manchester, 93; Newcastle, 93; Tynemouth, 93; York, 1831, 91, 92: 1844, 104
Brougham, Lord Henry, 42, 74
Buckland, William (1784–1856), 59, 62, 75
Butler, Dr., 42

Cambrian, 2, 71, 97, 100, 134
Cambrian–Silurian controversy, 74–85
Cambridge Conversazione Society. *See Apostles, The*
Cambridge Philosophical Society, 62, 89, 90, 108, 130, 133
Cambridge University 2, 4, 6, 11, 32, 38, 43–57, 61, 68, 74, 75, 86, 88, 90, 91, 102, 112–123, 125, 131–3, 138
   Colleges: Girton, 130; Queens', 55; St. Catharine's, 6; St. John's 36, 46, 55, 112; Trinity, 6, 15–18, 26, 32, 46, 47, 49, 52, **53,** 68, 103, 112, 132
Caradoc, 78, 81, 82, 97
Carboniferous, 36, 74, 75, 136
Catastrophists, 59, 60, 109
Chambers, Robert (1802–1871), 104–6, 108, 109, 125
Charles (Stuart), 26, 27
Cheshire salt mines, 61
Chester, Bishop of, 119
Clark, John Willis (1833–1910), 4
Cockburn, William (1773–1853), 104
Coleridge, Samuel T. (1772–1834), 87
Conybeare, William D. (1787–1857), 76
Cook, Captain James, 42
Cornwall, 62
Cowgill Chapel, 32, 126, **127,** 128, 129
Cumbria, 69, 136
Cuvier, Baron Georges L.C.F.D. (1769–1832), 59, 60, 104

Dales. *See* Yorkshire, Dales
Dalton, John (1766–1844), 47, 64, 65, 91, 95
Danby, Francis, 95
Darwin, Charles (1809–1882), 3, 98, 100, **101,** 102–111, 125, 133, 134
Darwin, Erasmus (1731–1802), 104
Dawson, John (1734–1820), 36–45, **44**
De la Beche, Sir Henry (1796–1855), 74, 75, 82

Index

Deluc, Jean A. (1727–1814), 58
Dent (inc. Dentdale), 1–5, 7, 8, **10,** 11, 13, 15, **16,** 17–19, 23, **30,** 32, 34, 35, 47–9, 51, 52, 72, 73, 95, 122, 126, 128, 129, 131, 136
Dent Grammar School, 6, 31, 33, 36–8
Derbyshire lead mines, 61
Deutscher Naturforsch Versammlung, 91, 92
Devon, 62, **76**
Devonian System, 2, 75, 76
Dorset, 62
Durham, 62

Ely, 94
Emerson, William, 42
Engels, Freiderich, 93, 94
Erickson, Erik (1902–   ), 51
Evans, Robert W., 55
Evolution, theory of, 102, 106, 108–111, 134

Farrer, J. W., 97
Foster family, 36
France, 52

Garsdale, 6, 39, 40, 43
Gay, John (1685–1732), 54
Geikie, Sir Archibald (1835–1924), 3, 67, 69, 71, 75, 83, 88, 89, 98, 121, 136
Geological Society of London, 56, 61, 65, 67–9, 75, 80–83, 89, 133
Geological Survey and Museum, 79, 81, 82
Germany, 52, 75
Gesellschaft Deutscher Naturforsch und Ärtze, 91, 92
Girton College. *See* Cambridge University
Gladstone, William E. (1809–98), 129
Gorham, George Cornelius, 55
Gough, Thomas, 64, 95, 97
Gray, Colonel, 119, 129

Hailstone, J. (1759–1847), 53, 54
Hall, Rupert, 89
Hallam, Arthur (1811–33), 88
Harcourt, Vernon, 91
Haygarth, John, 40
Henslow, John S. (1796–1861), 62, 89, 90, 100, 102
Heywood, J. 118
Horton-in-Ribblesdale, 6
Howitt, Mary (1799–1888), 6, 18
Howitt, William, 6
Hudson, J., 64
Hughes, T. McKenny (1833–1917), 4
Hull, Christopher (d. 1799), 38
Hutton, James (1726–1797), 58, 60, 62
Huxley, Thomas (1825–1895), 110

'Industrial Revolution', 18, 24, 25, 31, 60

Italy, 68, 69

Jameson, Robert (1774-1854), 47, 58, 100
Jones, Thomas, 46, 47
Jukes, Joseph B. (1811–69), 97, 98, 106

Kendal, 4, 17, 19, 21, 22, 27, 95, 138
Kendal Natural History and Scientific Society, 95, 96
Kirkby Lonsdale, 19, 63, 72, 73, 136
Kirkby Stephen, 19, 46

Lake District, 9, 25, 51, 63, 64, 69, 80, 136–8
Lamarck, Jean Baptiste de Monet (1744–1829), 85
Lapworth, Charles (1842–1920), 85
Lewis, T., 70
Llandeilo, 78, 82
London Mechanics Institute, 95
Lonsdale, William (1794–1871), 75
Lupton, Roger, 36, 38
Lyell, Sir Charles (1797–1875), 59, 60, 75, 106, 109, 124, 136

McCoy, Sir Frederick (1823–1899), 81
McCulloch, John (1773–1835), 62
Maillet, Benoît de (1656–1738), 104
Mason, Charles, 54
May Hill, 81, 84, 97
Michell, John (1724–93), 54
Miller, Hugh (1802–56), 94, 136
Murchison, Sir Roderick Impey (1792–1871), 3, 61, 67, 68, **69,** 70, 72, 75–9, 80–5, 91

Napoleonic Wars, 30, 47
Natural Theology, 4, 102, 111
Nelson, Viscount Horatio (1758–1805), 16, 38, 48
Neptunism, theory of, 58
Netherlands, 52
Newton, Sir Isaac (1642–1727), 42, 91
Nicholson, Cornelius, 95
Nicholson, Norman (b. 1914), 137, 138
Norwich, **10,** 32, 74, 75, 94, 123, 131, 132

Ogden, Samuel, 54
Origin of Species, 102, 106–9, 133, 136
Orton, 19
Osborne House, 116, 117, 119, 121
Otley, Jonathan (1766–1856), 63, 64, 138

Pagett, Maud, 125, 126
Paley, Archdeacon William (1743–1805), 102, 105
Parker, Mr., 9
Parliamentary Commission into the Universities, 1855, 120

144

Index

Peacock, George (1791–1858), 39, 46, 115, 119, 121
Peel, Sir Robert (1788–1850), 114–6, 118
Pennines, 62, 69, 136
Phillips, John (1800–1874), 62, 81, 91, 94
Playfair, John (1748–1819), 42, 47, 59, 60, 136
Plutonism, theory of, 59, 62
Powis, Lord, 112, 113
Priestley, Joseph (1733–1804), 47

Queens' College. *See* Cambridge University

Railways, 72, 126
  Kendal–Windermere, 96
  Settle–Carlisle, 32
Raistrick, Arthur, v, 1, 5, 19
Reform Bill 1832, 114
Religious Tests, Campaign against, 114, 115
Romilly, Sir J., 119, 121
Royal Commission into the Universities, 118–20
Russell, Lord John, 118, 119
Russia, 79

St. Catharine's College. *See* Cambridge University
St. John's College. *See* Cambridge University
Salter, J. W. (1820–69), 79
Sanders, Samuel (1746–82), 37
Scotland, 67, 68
Sedbergh, 8, 16, 17, 19, 25, 38, 41, 42, 45, 130
  School, 6, 36, **37**, 46; *see also* under individual masters
Sedgwick family
  Early forbears, 5, 6
  Adam, portraits **xii, 72, 135**
  Catherine Sidgwick, 8
  Isabella (1787–1823) (AS's sister), 8, 13, 14, 73
  John Sidgwick (AS's great grandfather), 6
  John (AS's brother), 8, 72, 73, 126
  Margaret Sturgis (AS's mother), 8, 73
  Margaret (AS's elder sister), 8, 49, 73
  Margaret (known as Isabella: AS's niece), 14, 117, 125, 130–2
  Parker (AS's Godfather), 9
  Richard (AS's father), 6, 9, 11–3, 18, 36, 38, 40, 73
  Richard (AS's nephew), 126
Sedgwick Museum, 82, 87, 132. *See also* Woodwardian Museum
Selwyn, Prof., 132

Sidgwick. *See* Sedgwick
Sills family, 13
Silurian System, 70, 71, 75–85, 123
Simpson, Thomas, 42, 48
Smiles, Samuel, 60
Smith, William (1769–1839), 53
Somerset, 62
Southey, Robert (1774–1843), 64, 95
Spencer, Herbert (1820–1903), 108
Staffordshire copper mines, 61
Stevens, W., 38, 39, 46
Stewart, Matthew, 42
Suffolk, 62
Switzerland, 52

Tennyson, Alfred Lord (1809–92), 87, 88, 105, 106
Thirlwall, Connop (1797–1875), 88, 115
Transmutation of species, 105
Trinity College. *See* Cambridge University
Tyrol, 68

Uniformitarianism, 59, 60, 109

Vale of Eden, 69
Victoria, Queen of England (1819–1901), 112, 114, 117, 119, 121, 122

Wales, 61, 70, 78, 79, 81, 83, 84, 91, 100–2, 134, 135
Wellington, Duke of, 16, 17
Werner, Abraham Gottlieb (1749–1818), 56, 62
Wharton, Posthumous (1674–1706), 37
Whewell, William (1794–1866), 59, 90, 112, 115, 121, 124, 132
Wilton, Richard (1827–1903), 87, 136
Woodward, Horace Bolingbroke (1848–1914), 81
Woodward, John (1665–1728), 53, 54, 88
Woodwardian Museum, 54, 98, 124, 131, 132; *see also* Sedgwick Museum
Woodwardian professorship, 54–57, 65, 74, 88, 97, 125; *see also* under names of professors
Wordsworth, C., 115
Wordsworth, William (1770–1850), 3, 9, 23–25, 44, 45, 63, 64, 87, 95, 96, 116, 137, 138
Yorkshire, 2, 32, 33, **66**, 69, 126, 132, 133
  Dales, 1, 2, 4, 5, 17, 19, 25, 33, 35, 44, 130
  Eastern, 62
  North, 62

Gritstone Publishing Co-operative Ltd

Gritstone Publishing Co-operative is Britain's first and so far, only writers' mutually owned publishing co-operative. Established in 2016 by four established Northern outdoor writers – Andrew Bibby, Chiz Dakin, Chris Goddard and Colin Speakman, the concept of the Co-operative is to support each member's writing and publishing activity with technical and marketing support. Members' publications can all be purchased via PayPal through the Gritstone website (www.gritstone.coop).

Whilst the Co-operative is not currently able to recruit new members, it is hoped that by setting up a new way of putting authors in charge at a time of unprecedented change in the publishing industry, including the rise of e-publishing, it is hoped that this will be a model open to other authors in future years. See the Gritstone website for further news.

GRITSTONE PUBLISHING